Dr. Don's Common Sense
Recipes for Relationships

Say "I Love You"
101 Ways How

Dr. Don Bartley

Say I Love You: 101 Ways How; Dr. Don's Common Sense Recipes for Relationships.

Copyright © 2013 by Don Bartley

Library of Congress Cataloging-in-Publication Data
Bartley, Don.
    Say I Love You: 101 Ways How; Dr Don's Common Sense Recipes for Relationships. / Don Bartley. – 1st ed.

ISBN 978-1493781898
    1. Self Help. 2. Relationships. 3. Family. 4. Love. 5. Affection.

Cover Design: Terry Locke

Printed in the United States of America.

I Give Thanks To:

Linda, my wife. She has loved me and put up with my quirks for decades. She is the best example I know, for how to love unconditionally. Her love tumbles out effortlessly as she goes about her day. Her life is a much better book on saying "I love you" than are my words.

Myssi, our daughter. Myssi is quick to give love and support, even to those who do not give it back. Her love and concern is expressed in many practical ways. She has a way of knowing what to do to help.

Dad and Mom. My earliest memories contain countless acts of love and care from Dad and Mom. Their lives seemed to revolve around taking care of the family. While not perfect, their love was obvious through acts and deeds as well as with words.

Roger, my brother. Roger has helped me take this writing from ideas to a readable work. He has also been a long time model of what I am trying to say. He is a true brother.

Terry Locke, my friend. Terry designed the cover of this book and his expertise has assisted me in completing the task. He has helped me to express my ideas accurately.

Friends and Family. There is a host of people throughout my life that have modeled the idea of giving love because it is the right thing to do. I remember college professors, friends, fishing partners, tennis partners, co-workers, etc., who show love with their very lives, actions, and attitudes.

Contents

36. Apologize
37. Sweep Out The Garage
38. Manage Your Tone Of Voice
39. Watch Your Body Language
40. Be A Friend
41. Stop
42. Go
43. Celebrate With Your Companion
44. Be Honest
45. Be Open
46. Kill Time Together
47. Listen
48. Laugh
49. Set Aside The Agenda
50. Break Bread Together
51. Value What Your Companion Values
52. Pray For Your Companion
53. Develop A Hobby Together
54. Shut Off Your Phone
55. Surprise Your Companion
56. Take Fun Pictures
57. Feed The Pets
58. Try Something New Together
59. Remember People Who Are Special To Your Companion
60. Provide A Romantic Atmosphere
61. Take Care Of The Car
62. Allow The Conversation To Meander
63. Go Visit Someone Together
64. Share Something you Have Learned
65. Dinner And A Movie
66. Plant Something Together
67. Kiss
68. Get Away From It All
69. Be A Gentleman/Be A Lady
70. Relax Together
71. Serve Each Other

72. Leave A Voice Message
73. Don't Continually Check To See If Your Companion Still Loves You
74. Dream Together
75. Talk It Out
76. Accept Your Companion For Who He Or She Is
77. Learn Self Control
78. Think Forward
79. Give The Look
80. Do Good Self Care
81. Manage Your Emotions
82. Allow For Flexibility
83. Step Back And Think
84. Get'r Done
85. Give Trust
86. Be Trustworthy
87. Look Into The Heart
88. Stay Out Of The Blame Game
89. Care About What Your Companion Cares About
90. Manage Your Attitude
91. Use Good Personal Hygiene
92. Give Respect
93. See Your Companion As A Person
94. Prepare A Warm Bath For Your Companion
95. Allow For Imperfection
96. Take Your Companion A Glass Of Tea
97. Don't Try To Fix Your Companion
98. Let Her Sleep
99. Pay Attention
100. Problem Solve
101. Get Help

Say "I Love You": 101 Ways How

Saying "I love you" goes a long way in keeping a relationship in good shape. In fact, those may be some of the most important words to come out of your mouth and, certainly, the most important to enter your ears. The experience of feeling loved is at the pinnacle of human experience. What could match that? Feeling loved can help us face the day and all that may accompany the daily grind. If things are good at home we can rise to the challenges that may come and celebrate the victories that we or those around us have. Feeling and being loved will carry the day.

Imagine going through the day without the basic love that you need. Even the neat things that you experience throughout the day, all around you, would not bring as much joy and happiness without love. Life would seem empty and hollow. It would feel like nobody really cares. While your achievements would be important, they would seem pointless. People who operate with the deficit of a loving atmosphere end up sad, lonely, and hopeless.

A sense of being loved is fundamental to a full human experience and goes a long way in giving meaning and purpose to life. Even animals flourish better in an atmosphere of care and love. How much more, humans need love and concern! Love is nutrition to the heart of humans and it's imperative that you find ways to express it to the people that you care about.

You must learn to tell them "I Love You", and tell them sincerely and often, if you hope to build and keep a relationship. Of course, say it in words, but beyond those words, there are a virtually endless number of other ways to say it as well. Words are important, but actions take love to a whole new level. This book will give some ideas for a variety of ways to say "I Love You" and to build your relationship. View these ideas as starters. Come up with a list of your own ideas, and express love as often as you can.

You will quickly catch-on to the idea that you'll need to become *intentional*, if you're to build a healthy relationship and keep it that way. This is not an exercise to be done for a mere few weeks or months, only to then be cast aside, feeling as though you've accomplished the task. It is a lifestyle to adopt and an attitude to build. It's about developing a mindset to keep you on track toward nourishing your relationship for all your years together. Consistently putting these ideas into practice will reap rewarding results for a lifetime!

Relationships are not rocket-science. Let's remove the complications and get down to the basics. Keep in mind that there are some fundamentals to put into place as you build your relationships. These fundamentals are: the right attitude, effective actions, and thoughtfulness. This book will assist you in implementing these fundamentals.

Throughout this book, I have chosen to use the word "companion" as a generic term to communicate the idea of spouse, partner, or any term you use in your relationship. Feel free to substitute your own term as you read on.

One of the most important goals is learning to develop a mentality and lifestyle of finding ways to communicate your love to those for whom you care. Don't leave it to chance or think that your companion "knows" that you love him or her. Show it by your words, actions and attitude. Here are 101 ways to get you started.

1. Embrace The Differences

Too often, after saying "I do", the unique characteristics of our spouse that enticed us so much early-on in our relationship become annoying and irritating. It's extremely important that we not let ourselves fall into the trap of simply *enduring* our differences. In fact, we should appreciate, value and capitalize on them. Differences can be very healthy for a relationship. The unique qualities in one of us can fill a hole in the other.

My wife is a perfectionist and she's great at tending to details. She always makes sure that things not only get done, but done *right* and on time. In contrast, I'm the big picture guy. Details drive me nuts. To get mired in details, on a daily basis, would make me a miserable person. Working together, we get it done right. She notices things that I may never see and thinks of things that would elude me, while I remain a stabilizing force, not getting lathered up about details.

Embracing our differences is not simply tolerating them; it's about recognizing the strengths in those differences and *utilizing* them. A difference with our companion doesn't mean there's something wrong with either of our views. We needn't develop the common habits of rolling the eyes and dismissively appeasing them. To simply "put up with it" is not only the wrong approach, it's a missed opportunity to have a truly great and mutually beneficial relationship.

2. Suspend Judgment

If you want to say I love you in a big way, learn to suspend judgment. Unfortunately, people are quick to judge and doing so will get you into untold trouble. Usually, it's not the act of rendering judgment that does the most damage, but the interpretation of it—how it's received.

If you are having surgery and your spouse does not show up for it, how would you feel? Would you feel like he does not care, or that you're not very valuable to him? But then, four hours later, you find out that he was in a terrible car accident. How does that now change how you feel? Your thoughts would likely shift radically.

It is wise to be patient, suspending judgment until all the evidence is presented. To achieve this, you'll need to become *intentional*. You must also truly believe in your companion. Otherwise, it will be difficult to suspend judgment. Learning to become intentional and believing in your spouse will go a long way in helping you to stop and think before jumping to conclusions.

Suspending judgment conveys the notion of trust in your companion and confidence that he/she will do the right thing and can handle situations. It's about giving the benefit of the doubt and patiently gathering information instead of assuming that you already know all there is to know.

Practice suspending judgment and you may discover that things will eventually turn out just fine.

3. Touch

Every human needs touch. Some are able to give and receive it naturally, while others find it awkward. Touch—one of the five senses—lends value to our body. Without touch, we can become self-conscious, believing that something's wrong with us.

The *kind* of touch is key. Sexual touch is fun, exciting and something we crave, but non-sexual touch sends a powerful message that we care about our companion in a more platonic, more thoughtful and less self-gratifying way. By nature, we tend to be self-serving. Non-sexual touching serves your companion and expresses no expectation in return.

Stereotypically, guys have more difficulty distinguishing and maintaining the barrier between sexual and non-sexual touch, instead following a straight path to a self-gratifying, sexual goal. Routinely doing so may shut down a girl's receptivity, leading her to the conclusion, "Okay, I know what he's after". There are many ways that nonsexual touching can be done without making her feel this way, such as holding hands, offering a warm embrace or simply touching her back as the two of you pass by in the house.

Try making touch a routine act of love. Consider what kind of touching your companion might like and develop a list of these ways so you can routinely express selfless love through touch.

4. Be Genuine

Who wants to be married to a fake? Do you? Neither does your companion. The opposite of fake, genuineness keeps you from looking over your shoulder and wishing you had done something differently. It lets you do it right the first time and have no regrets afterward.

Being genuine is about having character—being the *real deal*—sincere and honest. Genuineness constitutes what is best for a relationship, not simply what you want. It's about depth of character, rather than putting up a front or maintaining an image. Genuineness leaves no room for hypocrisy.

Being genuine is more than the saying "what you see is what you get". In fact, it's not about what you say at all. It's about being authentic and striving for excellence. It has the other person in mind, rather than being self-serving. It's not so much doing something out of a sense of duty, but because it is the right thing. It's about putting your heart into it and when you do that, your companion will sense it and really appreciate who you are.

Being genuine is more of a lifestyle than an act or achievement. It's an ongoing process of sincerity and thoughtfulness. If you're focused on self, you'll not likely be genuine. You'll be too obstructed by the selfish pursuit of your own desires. If you can focus instead on your companion's needs, you can provide for those needs with all sincerity and genuineness. Be the real deal!

5. Go For A Walk

Health care professionals commonly agree that walking is good for your health. However, there can be so much more to it than that. Walking can be a "two-fer" (two for the price of one). When you go for a walk together, you not only get the health benefits, but uninterrupted time together as well, which is a great relationship booster.

Regular walks together give you time to chat and engage in small talk that will connect you as a couple and, at the same time, render a little self-care. The meandering conversation can aid the body in relaxing and offer a rare opportunity for the mind to clear.

Walking lets you set aside, for just a little while, those things that tend to creep-in on conversations and sabotage them. There are no problems to solve during a walk, so just suspend the cares of the world for a little while as you stroll along. There will be plenty of time later to deal with pressing issues of the day. Just let those things go for awhile and bond with your companion. Notice the beauty, such as flowers, the terrain, the stars and planets, and yes, even the rain. Exchange some small talk and enjoy the presence of your companion.

Walk together, shut out the world for awhile and take a mental break. Use the time instead to pay attention to your companion. Simply being there and enjoying this time together will provide a prime opportunity to say "I love you."

6. Give Compliments

Does this dress make me look fat? Ever heard that one? What a trap! What are you supposed to say, "sure does" or "not really"? Compliments are a tricky thing. If given too often they lose their effectiveness, but if given too little they can sound manipulating (you must want something).

For compliments to be effective they need to be genuine and sincere. Half-hearted compliments won't go far, but you might be surprised to discover how easy it is to give genuine one. A simple "that was nice", or "that was really thoughtful", or "this meatloaf is really tasty", or "thank you for…" all communicate that you noticed something about your companion or what he/she did.

Being diligent with complimenting your companion also allows you to be honest when you need to convey a negative thought. For example, I have learned when asked if this "garment looks good on me" (one I don't like), to simply say "It's not your best color or doesn't give you the best look that you want. You make a lot of things look good but this might not be your best choice". I am both complimentary and honest, but also conveying the idea that this might not be a good choice for you. You needn't lie to be complimentary. Just the opposite is true; you will need to be honest and genuine.

Being complimentary is the simple act of communicating, in a helpful and honest way, what you notice. It has the best interest of your companion in mind.

7. Give Your Attention

There are a lot of things in life you can give, but none more important than your attention. Sometimes, when my wife and I are in a restaurant, I see people eating together that seem to never look at each other. They're not talking much and just not engaged in the moment. Not paying attention to one another seems to shout, "I DON'T CARE!" On the other hand, giving your companion attention seems to shout "I LOVE YOU!"

Attention expresses what you value. If you give all of your attention to a hobby, then you obviously value that hobby. If you're giving all of your attention to things or people other than your companion, you're sending the message that you don't value him/her very much.

I was once told by a person that she had tried to get her husband's attention so many times, but was unable to do so. One evening, while he was watching the game, she walked naked between him and the TV. As she was going by, he leaned over to look past her to see the play, not even noticing her. In what do you think he expressed more value? She went on to bed and cried herself to sleep.

Attention is a powerful thing. Where will you focus yours? Decide what is important to you and intentionally invest yourself in who or what that is. If you want to say I love you, then direct it toward your companion. Give the one you love the gift of attention!

8. Write A Love Note

Ah, the love note; the simplest of ways to say I love you without costing an arm and a leg. It's quick, simple, and packs a huge punch. You can *splurge* by writing a page or two to convey your inner thoughts, or just do a quickie and leave a post-it note with a meaningful message. It lets your companion know that you're thinking about him or her.

During a particular season in our life, I would be away for two weeks at a time. My wife, Linda, would strategically place notes in my pants pocket, the suitcase or even my shoes to remind me that she was thinking about me and to wish me a good day. Finding these notes, throughout my time away, meant a great deal to me. I'd carry them with me the entire time, occasionally reading them to stay in touch with her. It was a good "connecting point" while we were miles from each other. She'll also sometimes leave a note at home for me to find later, when I return home from fishing. Notes convey the notion that we care and are thinking of each other.

A love note can set the stage for a relaxed time when you're together and continue the loving feeling. It's beneficial for not only the one who receives it, but also for the one who gives it. There's something healthy that happens when you stop the world for a few seconds to convey your love to your companion. Saying I love you has a way of building even more love. It focuses attention and zeroes-in on the good, the beautiful, and the positive. So, go ahead, grab that pen and paper and say I love you.

9. Make Time For Your Companion

If you want time together, you'll have to *make it* or it won't happen. Many couples who come to me for pre-marital counseling are convinced that most of their problems will be solved *after* they marry, sure that they'll then have more time together. Unfortunately, I have to break the news that being married does necessarily guarantee more time together.

It seems like everything under the sun is vying for our time these days. So much to do, so many places to go, and so many people to see. Way too often, others seem to get our primetime, while our companions are left with the scraps. It's not so much about taking off, four days a week; it's more about stopping, listening and paying attention to each other.

Connect at the end of the day. Take time for just the two of you. Get away when you can, even when children are involved. Many couples haven't been alone together since their kids were born—sometimes in as much as seven or eight years! Before you know it, the years can slip by and you'll have missed many opportunities to connect.

And it's not just about long excursions or out-of-towners. When your companion needs you for something, try to be available. When he or she is talking, take time to listen. Marriages go stale and eventually die because people do not make time for each other. On the other hand, making that time for your companion is a powerful way to say "I love you".

10. Be Available

Availability sends a strong message. In the same regard, unavailability sends an equally strong, *opposite* message. When you're available to your companion, you communicate value in him or her. And, in turn, by being available, you become a valuable asset to your companion. Availability says that you think your companion is worthy of your time and presence, while *un*availability sends the message that you don't really care, leaving your companion to fend for themselves.

Availability comes in two main forms: presence and emotion. *Emotional* availability is about bringing yourself to the table as a real person with something to offer and not being closed off emotionally. The last thing your companion wants is someone he/she can't connect with or really know. It's also about being there when your companion shares his or her emotions. If you run every time something emotional comes up, then you're not emotionally available. Learn to not be afraid of your companion's emotions or to not try to quash them, but practice sitting with your companion through the emotions.

Presence is what all of us need—someone to be there for us and be available. We can be present in the conversation, present in the project, present at the special occasions of our companion, etc. Being present is more than physically showing up; it's being in touch and focused on your companion. Be there in attention and engagement.

11. Watch The Sunset Together

When we lived in Florida, one of our favorite things to do, and one of the most relaxing times we had, was to go to the gulf in the evening to sit and watch the sunset together. There was nothing else to do but wait for the sun to go down. It was romantic with nothing else added to it. You simply wait together, watching how the sunset will shape up and enjoying the time with each other, while noticing each unique sunset's blend of cloud configuration and atmosphere. It's an easy time with no agenda, allowing you to totally relax. That time in the evening will impact you like no other. It's truly made for lovers. It allows you to set aside all the activities of the day and seems to leave nothing else that matters but the moment.

While waiting to see the sunset, there will be ample time for casual conversation and enjoying each other's presence—a block of time with no agenda. Our world is so busy that it's easy to neglect that necessary down-time to just sit and think. Houses used to have front porches to facilitate this, or for folks to just sit and visit. Few houses now have them because people have moved away from the notion of just relaxing awhile and talking the evening away. There's too much to do, so we too easily forget about just being in the moment. Watching the sunset naturally provides that needed atmosphere to just be together with no other agenda. Lay the cares of the day down for a little while and be with the one you love. Relax, learn to be in the moment and let everything else just wait. Enjoy the sunset together.

12. Risk

Risk can be a good thing. Of course, foolish risk probably won't pan out so well. Healthy relationships include thoughtful risk, such as being hurt, embarrassed, a failure, disappointed or rejected. However, without risk, we'll never explore the depths of what a relationship can offer. Risk doesn't guarantee success or fulfillment, but it's necessary if we hope to have a healthy relationship.

Taking risks allows someone to get close enough to discover things about us that the average person doesn't know. Healthy relationships risk giving intimacy without receiving it in return, not being accepted or appreciated, not communicating very well or being misunderstood.

Risk is an everyday part of relationship. Without risk, we would simply close off and never be open enough for true intimacy. Are you covering up, hiding, or concealing parts of yourself for one reason or another? Do you allow your companion to carry the conversation because you are not willing to risk? If you're afraid to risk, you may be hindering the relationship from developing to its full potential. Unhealthy relationships sometimes reach the point where companions cease to take risks, or they create distances that hinder risk-taking.

Opening up to risk could keep your relationship alive and vibrant. Risk revealing who you are. You might discover that your companion wants you to just to be yourself. Risk meandering in conversation or just dreaming together and see where it takes you. Risk giving and receiving intimacy. Have some fun as you learn to take risks. Taking risks together says I love you.

13. Don't Compare

Comparison is a landmine and will surely have serious repercussions. Your companion is one-of-a-kind. Sure, there are patterns and we would be wise to learn and appreciate that fact, but each of us is unique in some way. Not even identical twins are exactly alike, even if you can't tell them apart. Learn to see your companion as unique and appreciate the exclusive qualities that he or she offers.

Neither gender wants to be compared to others, nor do we like our work or performance to be compared to others. Just as no child likes to hear "Why can't you be like your brother?, our companion doesn't want to hear something like "You sure can't cook like my mom" or "Why can't you be thoughtful like Jim?"

If you want to communicate the notion "I love you" to your companion, then don't compare. See him or her as a person with unique character clusters and appreciate the uniqueness. No other person embodies the special qualities like those of your companion.

My favorite movie of all time is "It's A Wonderful Life", wherein Jimmy Stuart's character, George, got so low in life that he wished he'd never been born. Clarence the Angel granted his wish and he experienced how life would have turned out if George had never been born. This movie is a powerful message about what life would be like without each of us and our impacts on each other. We are *all* important. We forget that sometimes. Maybe it's time to see your companion through a whole different lens and appreciate what he or she contributes to life. Don't compare; just value.

14. Pick Strawberries Together

...or apples, or blueberries, or whatever you like. Sounds like work to me. Personally, I'd rather swing by the farmers market, pick up the strawberries, put them in the cooler, go sit down where it is cool and have a bite of lunch. After all, it's hot out there and the bugs are biting! Yes, I sometimes whine a bit and complain about "not having time for this." I must admit, I dread going out in the heat to pick *anything*. I think I did that too much when I was growing up and it doesn't appeal to me as a pleasurable experience.

There are rewards though. It's something you can do together and, if you have kids, they can really make things fun (or at least interesting). At the end of the adventure, you have some of the freshest and healthiest products you can find. To top it off, you've also achieved something together and have a real sense of accomplishment. We've picked coolers full of blueberries, put them in the freezer and had blueberry pies and smoothies for months. We've picked bucketfuls of apples and had apple pies and even *fried* apple pies for months. Yum, yum! The payoff lasts a long time and is a continual reminder of what we have achieved together. So, I just get my butt out there and do it.

For you, it may be planting flowers or doing lawn work together. Maybe it's hiking in nature or going for a bike ride. Maybe it's stopping by the farmers market. Whatever it may be, find what works for you. Get out there and do something together. Achieving things together will say a warm "I love you."

15. Take Care Of Business

There are lots of things that must be done and maintained in a long-term relationship. Taking care of business ranges from the urgent and extremely important to the mundane and trivial, but in the big scheme of things, *all* are important. It may be paying a bill or simply wiping off the counter top when you're finished making a sandwich. Regardless, take care of it and don't procrastinate.

It gets really irritating in a relationship if one person is not pulling his or her share of the load and shifting responsibility to the other. It sends the message, "I don't really care all that much about what you want." It may seem like something that's trivial to you, but it may be really important to your companion. A molehill to one person can be a mountain to the other.

Taking care of business also means being proactive. It's irritating when a person procrastinates and never seems to get things done. You'll need to notice what needs to be done and not wait to be asked to do it. Learn to see these things for yourself.

Figure out what it takes to run your household. Tend to the business aspects of life. Look for the little things as well as the huge things. Learn to maintain as you go and don't let it all pile up. Finish the job and, when you do, put the tools away and clean up the mess. Take care of things as they come up and don't put them off. Taking care of business tells your companion "I love you."

16. Be Your Companion's Greatest Fan

We live in a world full of athletes, actors, artists and other famous people. Fans go ape over them. While your companion may be "just a regular person", one of the best things you can do is be their greatest fan. Those famous people are not with you every day, but your companion is. They don't have to put up with your quirks, but your companion does. They don't need you, personally, to be their fan, but your companion does.

It's very personal with your companion. Sure, others could be a fan to your companion, but their admiration is not nearly as meaningful as *yours*. Others can compliment me, but when my wife compliments me it is the most meaningful compliment on the planet.

Your companion doesn't need to accomplish something world renown for you to be his/her fan. They just need to be who they are. I love my wife for who she is. She doesn't need to be like anyone else; she just needs to be herself.

A false notion is that we have to be the best. We don't. Simply allow your companion to be themselves and learn to appreciate who they are and the qualities that he or she embodies. When you practice that principle, you'll notice all sorts of things that you value and admire about your companion. Nature will take you down the road toward complaints and criticisms. However, if you learn to be your companion's greatest fan, you'll watch his/her positives shine and their negatives lose relevance.

17. Be Thankful

Have you noticed the amount of ungratefulness in the world today? Sometimes, it seems that people expect too much and are way too self-centered. They complain a lot, for some reason, and fill the world with criticism.

One day, I noticed that I'd slumped into the habit of not giving thanks. For example, Linda would bring a glass of tea or refill the glass and I'd say nothing. However, at a restaurant, I'd say thanks to the waitress who did the same thing. That didn't seem quite right. As I thought about it, I noticed that I took Linda and the generous things she did for granted. I began to notice how many ways I'd failed to show thankfulness or gratefulness. I made changes immediately and found out that just a little thankfulness goes a long way.

It's easy to make thankfulness a part of your everyday life by developing the art of noticing what your companion contributes and communicating thankfulness. A quick "thank you" communicates that you noticed. Complimenting something your companion has done is a genuine way to express thankfulness. Thankfulness is an attitude—a way of thinking. I have a neighbor who likes to say "that is the best I ever had" just about every time he eats something delicious. The really neat thing about that is that he means it. He truly enjoys good food or dessert. He's a great example of someone who's thankful. You can tell that he means what he says, and he's quick to say it because he notices. Thankfulness sends an important message to your companion.

18. Play Together

When we first meet, it's easy to play together. After we get busy in life, we often tend to forget about taking the time to do that. Playing is so much fun in the beginning and, in reality, we don't have to work hard at it because it comes so naturally. But then the reality of life begins to set in and responsibility consumes us.

There is a time to work and a time to play. Too many times, we get caught up in adulthood and life and forget to play. I think we're happy when we work hard, but we also need that playtime. How long has it been since you've played a board game or a card game? Recently, we played a game with friends in which we had to make up sentences from random words. At times, we'd be laughing so hard that we couldn't even read the sentence aloud.

There are many ways to play. It doesn't always have to be a store-bought game; you can have fun doing just about anything. Playful moments can come at any time, so just be open to it and make it a point to have some fun.

Playing is as much an attitude as an event. If you let life take over, things will get way too serious. Learn to laugh at yourself and with others. Playing will actually build energy. Dive in and get involved in a little clean fun. You'll notice your energy level begin to rise.

There is something really healthy about playing and laughing together. Take care of the responsibilities, but then turn loose for a little fun with your companion. Having fun together is a really cool way of saying I love you.

19. Manage Money Well

I know, I know, this is a painful subject. "Budget" is a dirty word in many households. We keep it all in our heads when it comes to money. We can juggle it, no problem. Right? Not usually.

People fight over money way too much. Financial problems are a huge issue for many couples. However, there's a better way. You can manage money well and take the fighting off the table in your relationship. Sometimes savers marry spenders and vice versa. One person focuses on saving for the future, making sure money will be available for the kid's college or retirement, while the other focuses on living a little now. One has to have everything he/she wants *now*, while the other can wait.

It comes down to a few fundamental principles and putting those to work consistently. There are several professionals who teach balanced money managing strategies that work. Study those principles and let them guide you in managing your money well.

Instead of bickering about financial matters, learn to discuss them and to find some common ground. Learn to live within your means without overspending. It takes discipline to forgo things you might like, in order to keep yourselves financially secure and stable. Debt is a huge budget killer. Get together with your companion to develop a financial plan that will incorporate both of your concerns. If you will manage your money well, you'll take much of the tension out of your relationship. It takes patience, work and thought to develop and maintain an effective money-management strategy.

20. Tell Her How Beautiful She Is

A long time ago, while I was in college, an old professor, whom I respected very much, would yell across campus and ask, "Bartley, have you told your wife today how beautiful she is?" Of course, you couldn't lie to him because God would strike you dead if you did. I would reply, "No, not yet". He would then respond, "go and tell her right now." And so, I would. Finally, I figured out that it was better to tell her *before* I left home.

An interesting thing began to happen when I told her every day how beautiful she was. I saw her become even *more* beautiful as a result. And she continues to be beautiful to this day. Being diligent in telling your companion how beautiful she is, you'll notice your attraction build. You'll see features that you previously missed or ignored. It does something within you.

It also does something in your companion. It helps her to find and accept her beauty. Each person is beautiful in many ways, but for some it takes time for them to accept and grasp it. You can help this along by communicating the beauty you see in her.

Recognizing and communicating beauty helps us to keep things in perspective. For some reason, it's easy to see the flaws in each other, but more difficult, day-to-day, to notice the beauty. The negative aspects and quirks stand out, while beauty is often quiet and unassuming. However, when you make a practice of noticing and appreciating that beauty, you'll discover that you're not nearly as quick to point out the flaws. Make a point to regularly notice the beautiful and the positive in your companion.

21. Do The Dishes Together

Believe it or not, doing the dishes together can be a time to relax and touch base for the day. The dishes need to be done anyway, so why not jump in and get the job done together? Table time can be very rewarding, and the cleanup time can be just as valuable. This is a time when you can catch up on the small talk and generally check in with your companion to see how he or she is doing. Often, it's during small talk that we connect the best.

Don't be so focused on making sure everything is perfect. Just try to focus on the relationship and let the small stuff go. I know hundreds of couples that have bickered over how to load a dishwasher. Does it really matter that much? There is one rule of thumb: the knife points go down. Outside of that, not much else matters.

When the two of you take on a task of some sort, you'll have an opportunity to engage in casual conversation that can let you touch base and connect with each other. Grab every opportunity possible to spend time together. It's not so much about the task as the time you have together in a casual way. You don't have to solve the world's problems, but you can enjoy each other for a few minutes. These moments together are not optimally spent in solving problems or giving advice.

Make opportunities to connect with each other. If you focus more on the task than connecting with each other, you may not enjoy the experience nearly as much. So relax as you do the dishes and enjoy the evening together.

22. Forgive

Forgiveness is a must in a relationship. Invariably, we will hurt one another or irritate each other. Without forgiveness, the relationship can get damaged with hurts and heartaches.

Forgiveness is an accounting term that simply takes the deed off the account. Forgiveness acknowledges that what your companion did was wrong, but volunteers to take the offense off the account and treat it as it no longer exists. Forgiveness doesn't justify the deed, nor does it allow the person to keep doing the same damage. Forgiveness simply takes the record of the deed off the account.

The cliché "forgive and forget" is not possible for us humans. God can forget, but we mere mortals are wired to retain the memory. Forgetting is a nice idea, but not realistic. It's more like we forgive and *remember*. It would be nice to remove it from memory altogether, but sadly it's there to stay. However, we can turn it loose and move on in life to a better place. We can turn the hurt loose as well. When you let it go, you'll discover a freedom that you didn't have before. Carrying the offense hurts you more than it hurts the offending person.

In life, there will be a million (not an exaggeration) things to hurt, offend, or make you mad. Forgiveness keeps you from carrying those offenses with you forever. It sets you free to love and to avoid bitterness. Make a practice of forgiveness. Learn to let offenses go, move on, and enjoy life.

23. Walk In The Snow Together

Even simple things like walking together in the snow will provide a quiet time with each other. Not long ago, Linda and I went for a walk while it was snowing and experienced a tranquility that was not possible on other days. Not much was stirring, and there was no one to interrupt the walk or conversation. In the silent air, there was a peacefulness that made the walk relaxing.

Normally, we talk as we walk, but this time we focused on the tranquility. This walk was more relaxing than the usual ones. It seemed like walking in the snow removed any distractions and let us have the peacefulness to ourselves. I wonder what walking in the rain would do. Oh, we've done that too. You might want to try it sometime; it's an experience like no other. I won't spoil it for you, but let you venture out and give it a try...when there's no lightning, of course. In that case, walking turns to running.

After taking a walk in the snow together, we talked about how long it had been since we'd last done that. It was quite a romantic outing. I'm sure the neighbors described it a little differently, but we had a ball.

Learn to be open to different ideas and explore them to see if they'll work for you. Of course, keep safety in mind, but live a little and be open to something different. Think outside the box some and mix it up a little. People may think you're crazy, but you'll have a blast. Use your imagination to see if you can come up with some tranquility of your own.

24. Support Your Companion

If you fail to remain alert, you'll support everyone but your companion. When your companion tells of some outside event that hurt or was frustrating, it's tempting to assess the situation and make your own assumptions and interpretations as to what occurred. Your intent may be to help your companion see the event in another light so it doesn't hurt so much. That's noble, but it backfires. Your companion may not feel supported by you; he or she may feel as though you're taking the other person's side. That's not your intention, but in the eyes of your companion you failed to support him/ her. They're looking for your support, not necessarily your explanation, approval or advice. Sometimes, your companion may want to express these frustrations just to get it off their chest. The best thing to do is listen and offer support. It's not about agreeing or disagreeing; it's about caring and listening.

You'll also want to learn to support your companion by taking an interest in what he/she likes. There's no need to do *everything* your companion likes doing, just support their interests. I fish, but my wife does not. She supports my hobby with gift cards and making sure I have time to enjoy it. She doesn't nag or complain about it. And when I get back from fishing, it's time to shift the focus to *her* interests.

Support runs in both directions. And when you lend it, you send a strong message that you care and believe in your companion. You can start the ball rolling with your support.

25. Learn Some Patience

Patience is difficult sometimes, but impatience makes matters worse. If you get frustrated and lose your temper, you'll put distance between you and your companion. If it leads further downhill to slamming or throwing things, you'll send a message to your companion that it's not safe to be with you.

On the contrary, developing and demonstrating patience creates a safe environment and tells your companion that it's okay to be with you. Keeping your head in tough situations will help you to make better decisions and, normally, get better outcomes.

Developing patience requires that you learn to change how you think, look at things differently and make a habit of stepping back and seeing the big picture. In the larger scheme of things, you can see how it might be alright in the long run. Also, realizing that not *all* situations can go well helps to gain a different perspective. The more you accept this, the more your patience will grow.

Sometimes, you just roll with it, knowing that tomorrow will be better. The intensity of the moment might be frustrating, but know that you'll get through it. The sun will still come up tomorrow. If you can learn to roll with the punches, life might get a little easier.

A really neat by-product of developing patience is that it develops a good atmosphere with your companion.

26. Shop Together

Early in our marriage, I would have sworn that the floors in shopping malls were built with material that massaged the legs of women, but caused the legs of men to ache. After all, I had proof: Linda was happy and took her time while shopping, but I was miserable, my legs ached, and I just wanted to get out of there, fast. It wasn't until later that I realized the difference: Linda is a browser and I am a hunter.

Linda would go into the store, take her time and browse, while I would scan the place, head straight for what I wanted, bag it, and drag it home. I like tearing it out of the package and using it. Linda, on the other hand, enjoys the browsing experience and doesn't have much desire to bag anything; she just enjoys looking at it. Browsing makes no sense to me.

One day, while Linda was browsing, I performed an experiment. I stepped to the rack where she was browsing and when I found a color and cut I liked, I pulled it out, held it up and said, "Isn't that cute?" Linda replied, "It sure is." I then hung it back on the rack. Never before had I done that. If it is the right color, the right cut, and the right size, I bag it and drag it out. But, this time, it was different. I discovered something: It wasn't the event of bagging it that was important to Linda; it was enjoying the experience together. That day, I stopped looking at my watch and leaning on shelves as if to say "are you ready to go?" I learned to enjoy the experience with her and enjoy the pleasure that it brings to her. Shopping with Linda has become one more way I can say "I love you."

27. Work In The Yard Together

Many people over the years have told me that yard work is therapeutic for them. I've told most of them that if they want some extra therapy, they can come over and work in my yard. They laugh, but so far, nobody has come by with a mower or weed-eater. I suspect that only *your own* yard qualifies as therapeutic.

For some, yard work is a way of relieving the built up tension of the week, and the smell of fresh cut grass is a reward all its own. It's also a way of keeping your nest in good order and having some healthy pride in what you have. For some, their nest reflects their own identity and, therefore, they see a need to keep it in good order. There are tangible results that you immediately see as you look over what you've completed. You receive immediate feedback as you keep up the lawn. Planting flowers and trees beautify, is good for the environment, and it makes you feel good after completion. Achieving these projects together gives you a sense of accomplishment and well-being.

There is benefit in getting out in the fresh air and enjoying the outdoors. Fresh air is a lifter of the mood and lends to a positive sense of contentment. There's also much benefit from the physical workout that yard work provides.

When you complete yard work together you will build a sense of teamwork as well as achieving something you can see. Doing the job together has a way of building positive connection as a couple. Go ahead, get out there and have fun planting, trimming, clipping, fertilizing and pruning!

28. Cook A Special Meal

Preparing someone's favorite dish is like speaking the words "I love you" through a megaphone. You have to invest time, energy, and thoughtfulness to get the ingredients together and cook the meal. You have your companion in mind from the very beginning.

For some people, it doesn't have to be all that special. Just preparing something that he or she likes is special enough. Nor does it have to be a gourmet meal, but only something your companion likes. For those who live in such a hurry, sometimes just about any sit-down meal would be nice. It conveys the notion that you care.

Another twist is to cook the meal together. Early in our marriage, we'd sometimes get up in the wee hours of the morning to cook eggs, bacon, gravy and biscuits. We'd eat and go back to bed. Man, those were the years! Time spent cooking together can be relaxing and connecting. It's a time to casually catch up and enjoy each other's presence. Don't worry if the dishwasher isn't loaded the way you like, or if everything is just right. It probably won't be. But you can have a good time together. That's worth it all. Food is a great connector. Just ask your friends or the people at church. Table time can be really rewarding.

Preparing a favorite meal for your companion is not about a sense of duty; it's more about a sense of thinking about your companion and wanting to do something nice for no reason at all. It's about "I want to" versus "I need to". If you see it as just one more responsibility, you'll not grasp what great joy there is in doing something nice for your companion.

29. Pay Attention To Your Companion In Public

It's easy to take each other for granted or neglect each other in public. We get busy with friends and events and forget to notice what our companion needs. If you're the talker, you might get so caught-up in the audience that you don't even notice that your companion is all alone and cannot find the way into a conversation or group. Yes, we're there for others, but we can also be there for each other.

Paying attention to your companion in public doesn't mean that you must ignore others or that the two of you are all about yourselves. It means that you *include* your companion, that you are aware of their needs. You don't have to *choose between* as much as you need to *include*.

Paying attention can mean many things. It can be listening, including in activities or conversation, noticing needs or knowing when it is time to go. It can also mean that you share the floor, listen to your companion and value what he or she contributes. If you'll pay attention, you will learn to read your companion and know what to do. And you'll need to set aside your agenda, in order to read your companion. If you're caught up in your own thing, it's not likely that you'll pay much attention to him/her.

Paying attention to your companion in public doesn't have to be something huge. It can simply be that warm look across the room. It also doesn't mean that you two fall all over each other in public. However, it does mean that you notice and connect with each other. Paying attention to your companion in public can send a warm "I love you."

30. Take Out The Trash

There's sort of a double meaning to this one. On the one hand, we need to physically take out the trash. On the other, we need to figuratively do so.

In the literal sense, we have a little custom at our house: we take out the trash every day so it won't stink. I'm not talking about just taking out the trash, exclusively. I'm getting at the idea of doing the little things without being asked or pushed, or letting them pile up. There are a million little things that, if viewed on their own, probably doesn't make all that much difference. However, when they accumulate, they make a bigger statement. By tending things regularly and thoughtfully, you make a statement that you care and are willing to be part of the team. All of us produce trash and it needs to be taken out regularly. All of us contribute to the little things that accumulate around the house and we each need to be a part of tending them.

In the figurative sense, we also produce trash in our relationships, from time to time, and it needs to be taken out as well. There are things we don't get quite right or that we might botch up really badly. If so, take out that trash too. Be willing to own your part and to make things right. When you make a mistake, own it and don't point your finger at your partner. Getting defensive only makes it worse. Own it and do something about it. Taking responsibility for the relationship sends a message that you really care. Develop a routine of paying attention to what needs to be done and doing it without being asked or reminded.

31. Go To Church Together

Going to church together has been a huge plus in our marriage. It's helped us to grow together, get closer to God, and re-calibrate our lives with Him. As our spiritual lives have strengthened, our relationship has deepened. God has a way of keeping us on track and teaching us what's important.

Church has been a great resource for finding good friends that we've enjoyed over the years, many of which have become our true friends for life. Our daughter grew up with their kids and we've collected many fond memories along the way.

The church has also provided a great vehicle for us to serve and to touch our community. It's there that we've found our own way and been able to help others find theirs. It provides for us a great way to make a real difference and be involved in something bigger than ourselves.

Not to say that it's perfect. You will, no doubt, find imperfect people there who are trying to find their own way and, through sharing that experience, will help you to find your own as well. Since finding God, we've dedicated our lives to share with others. We see church as a privilege. We don't *have* to go, we *get* to go.

The undeniable truth is that the church and the Bible have instilled in us the most wholesome principles by which we live. These principles are for all time. We can rest assured that they'll continue to work for us today and forever.

32. Go Out For A Piece Of Pie

A co-worker and I would periodically go out for a cup of coffee and a piece of pie, for no reason, just to do it. It was over a piece of pie that the conversation played out in its own unique way. The pie and coffee was just the board and the time together was the chalk. Subjects came up, plans developed, and friendship built. There was no wondering where each other stood on issues; we knew because we'd come to know each other at a deeper level. There was a camaraderie that developed and a brotherhood evolved.

Oddly enough, as much as I like meatloaf, I'm not sure it would have achieved the same results as pie. The pie was a treat—totally unnecessary. Therefore, I think that element aided in the feeling of having "no agenda", allowing the conversation to meander in its own course.

Taking the time to set aside the world for awhile and enjoy the presence of another person can make a huge difference. If you and your companion were to routinely get together over a piece of pie (or anything you like) and just let the conversation evolve, you'll be surprised at how you'll develop a deeper understanding and appreciation for one another. The cares of the day will always be there, but just take a break from them and enjoy the time with your companion.

Find a mode that will help you set aside the cares of the world so you and your companion can relax together. Don't like pie and coffee? Find something that the two of you like. You might just find your own chalkboard.

33. Be Careful With Assumptions

Assumptions can get you in trouble quickly. I once worked in a bookstore. One day, while the other staff was out to lunch, I was running the check out. As it normally would, a line formed as I fell behind. A nice young lady stepped forward with her selections. It was obvious to me that she could give birth any minute, so I asked her when she was due. She replied, "I'm not pregnant!" As luck would have it, everyone in line behind her was female and they all heard the conversation well. I could sense their eyes burning a hole right through me. The keys on the cash register clicked a lot faster after that, and the following conversations were cold. I'm not exactly sure who was out to lunch, the staff or me. Let me say it again: assumptions can get you in trouble quickly. I don't ask that question anymore.

Assumptions are easy to make and come naturally because they seem reasonable. I've heard many say that "perception is reality". I say that perception is just perception. It may be far from reality. Honestly, she looked full-term pregnant to me. *That* perception was definitely not reality. I made an assumption, but wished to God that I hadn't done so.

Do you assume that you know best, or that you're right? If you find yourself quickly jumping to conclusions, you may be operating on assumption. One way to cut down on assumptions is to listen well enough to fully understand the experience of your companion—to get to the bottom of what's being communicated. Be very careful with those assumptions.

34. Be Kind

One powerful way to say "I love you" is to be kind to your companion. Kindness shows fondness, whereas harshness shows contempt. Who really wants to be spoken to in harsh, uncaring tones or words? The last person that your companion needs harshness from is you. It's easy to fall into the trap of not paying attention to how you talk to, or relate to, your companion. We get busy and neglect to notice how we come across to each other. Sometimes, there is so much to get done that we don't take the time to be kind; we just want to get it done.

Kindness requires thoughtfulness. And, because life sometimes gets frustrating, you'll need to be intentional, in order to be kind. Study how you come across to your companion. Listen to your tone of voice. Notice your body language. Evaluate *what* you say and *how* you say it. Are you kind? Would your companion tell others how kind you are? You'll need to stay alert, if you hope to be kind. There are so many frustrating things in life. We often have knee-jerk reactions to frustrating situations. Bad reactions to frustrating situations are not usually kind to anyone. If you stay alert, you can relate to your companion in ways that will pull you together, rather than pushing you apart. You can speak in ways that you won't later regret.

Kindness starts with the right attitude. If kindness doesn't matter very much to you then you'll likely come across as blunt and uncaring. If you truly care about your companion, you will likely show kindness. Stay alert, pay attention and let your words, tone of voice and body language say "I love you" through an attitude of kindness.

35. Bring A Gift From A Trip

The romantics have it all over the rest of us. They seem to naturally know the right thing that will wow their companion. But the rest of us sometimes don't give it a second thought or, in my case, even a first. At times, it just doesn't occur to some of us that we ought to do something. It's like the old farmer whose wife was starved for him to say "I love you". He said that he'd told her forty years ago that he loved her and, if that ever changed, he'd let her know.

There are ways of saying "I love you" with a simple gift. Bringing a gift back from a trip communicates to your companion that you thought about him or her while you were away. It wouldn't work if I brought a fishing lure to Linda. I'd be wiser to bring something that she enjoys. It is not the size or price of the gift nearly as much as the thought behind it. If you ignore your companion's interests, it's obvious that you're not really thinking about them; you're just checking something off the list. It requires a little thought. It's also not wise to wait until the last minute to pick up something because procrastination will just increase your odds of a thoughtless selection.

One of the best ways to do well in gift giving is to pay attention to your companion's interests. If you really know your companion, you'll have a deeper understanding of what's appropriate. There are some that, instead of a gift, would prefer having some consistent contact while you're away. Learn your companion's preferences and you'll know what to do.

36. Apologize

A good apology is a lost art these days. It seems like it's always someone else's fault. The truth is that none of us do it all just right. We're just not that good. Sometimes, we miss the mark by a mile and hurt each other's feelings. I know some people that probably have never said "I'm sorry". It seems that nobody can remember them saying it without a qualifier, such as "I'm sorry, *but* this is the way it is." That's not an apology.

Sometimes a good apology is in order. If you want an apology to count, you must be genuine and honest about it. A hang-dog "sorry" doesn't cut it. It must come from the heart, if it is to be felt by the other person. One of the best ways to ensure that is to genuinely appreciate the extent of wrong or hurt that you caused and grasp how it must have felt to the other person. If you don't know or care what you've done, you will not likely present a heartfelt apology. View the issue and hurt from the perspective of your companion—empathize—and set aside your own logic for the moment.

If you really care about how your companion feels, you'll need to learn to apologize when necessary. What you don't want to do is to apologize all the time simply to appease your own self-esteem issues, nor do so flippantly so that it has no real meaning. The key is to offer an apology when one is in order and make it heartfelt and genuine. Learn to issue a meaningful apology when needed and let your companion know you're genuinely sorry for hurting him or her.

37. Sweep The Garage

Sweeping the garage can seem trivial. When my wife steps out of her car after I've swept the garage, there is no "crunch" when her foot hits the floor. It makes her feel good about the "nest" we live in. Sweeping the garage is an idea that's bigger than just cleaning up. It's not so trivial to her; it communicates that I care.

When you tend to the little things, you project to your companion that you care enough to take notice and to tend to both big and small things alike. Failing to tend to the little things sends a message that you really don't care. Sweeping the garage, hosing off the patio, picking up through the house, returning calls, being on time and other actions communicate that you care about your companion.

What's really a downer is when you tend to things you like and want with great detail, but you let things that your companion considers important slide. This happens way too often. There is so much more motivation to get engrossed in the things we like to do and not nearly as much motivation to tend to things we don't like so well. Both have a huge amount of importance.

I doubt that we'll ever have equal motivation and excitement for all things. I admit to you that I am eager to go fishing, but not equally as eager to weed-eat. It's not really about the excitement level, even though we need to have a good attitude about doing it. Instead of saying to myself, "Let me sweep out the stupid garage", with a good attitude, I just sweep out the garage. It doesn't help to sulk and throw things because something is unpleasant; just keep a good attitude and do it.

38. Manage Your Tone Of Voice

Tone of voice communicates volumes! It can pack a much bigger punch than the words that are uttered. Here's where I need a mechanism, like one of those musical cards from the card store, to get the idea across. I don't have that mechanism, so we'll just have to use our imagination.

Imagine for a moment that your companion says in a warm and friendly tone, "I love you". Now imagine those same words in a heated moment right after a fight, when you're trying to make up. Your companion says with an edge, "I LOVE YOU!" It makes you want to laugh, doesn't it? Same words, but different feel to the message.

Perhaps one of the biggest blunders we make is that we don't slow down enough to actually send the message that we intend. We're in a hurry, or life gets in the way, and we just blurt out what is on our mind. We think it will come across just fine, but it doesn't. Our companion is upset and we look across the room and say, "WHAT?" We have no idea what just happened.

It may be that your tone of voice was not consistent with your words. You have a choice with that tone, but in order to use it, you'll need to stop and think before speaking. You'll need to be thoughtful about making sure you convey what you really mean. It is better to *say* "I am upset", rather than letting your tone of voice say it for you. It's a mixed message to say one thing, while your tone of voice conveys something completely different. It's difficult for your companion to determine which message you're really emphasizing, so manage your tone of voice.

39. Watch Your Body Language

Just as tone of voice is a powerful thing, so is body language. It sometimes "tells on us". It tells when we are frustrated or angry. It tells when we are afraid or sad. Our body language sends messages to others about what's going on inside of us. It sometimes sends messages that we would really prefer not to send. It's not always intentional, but it happens, and it may be inconsistent with our spoken words.

When irritated, frustrated, or put-off about something, some people roll their eyes. When disgusted, fed up, or hacked off, some people huff or sigh deeply. These and other sorts of body language send a clear message that we don't like what's going on. Sometimes, we react to the other person's body language and make matters worse.

Become intentional about the messages you send in body language. Notice whether you look your companion in the eye or you tend to look away. Notice whether you sit in an open posture to your companion or whether you close off. Notice whether you have a defensive attitude or whether you are open. Is your animation sending a positive message or are you flat and showing disinterest? Your body language is sending some message, so become intentional about what you want to convey.

Keeping an open and accepting attitude will go a long way in helping you to manage your body language. It all starts by accepting your companion and having the attitude that you'll work through issues together.

40. Be A Friend

What a blessing it is when your companion is your best friend. The best way to *have* a friend is to *be* a friend. Think about what it takes to be a friend. It means remaining aware of what is going on and having the other person's best interest at heart. It means sometimes setting aside your own needs to tend to those of your friend. It's about getting through the tough times together and celebrating the good times. We work and play together, laugh and cry together, push forward and relax together, enjoy each other, and get irritated with each other. Life throws many things at us, but we face them together. That's what friends do. It's not a perfect relationship, but it's one that endures and considers the needs of both parties.

Sometimes, after being in a relationship for awhile, people forget to be a friend and assume that the other person will always be there. That's when we get sloppy, are not intentional, and treat our companion poorly. This is the very reason many relationships break apart. They let the friendship go stale and fail to tend the very thing that brought so much joy in the first place. Little by little, the fire dies out and, before long, people get snappy with each other and fail to act like friends. If you let the friendship die out, you'll eventually wind up with a troubled relationship.

It's imperative that you tend the friendship and keep it alive and vibrant. Think about what your companion likes and needs and then have some fun tending those things together. Keep working on your friendship; it will pay dividends for a lifetime.

41. Stop

Sometimes, we just need to stop. I've seen a guy joke with his wife and take it so far that it ends up making her furious. It could have been a nice moment with some lighthearted humor, but he didn't recognize when to stop. I've seen people go too far in conversation, leading to hurting each other. I've seen behavior that irritates the daylights out of a companion and bad habits that push them away. I've also seen laziness that makes the relationship become a heavy load to drag around.

The solution, of course, is to stop the behavior that's hurting your relationship. The excuse, "I can't stop" won't work; it will just perpetuate unwanted results. You have total control over your behavior, so stop those that are not good for your relationship. In order to do so, you'll first need to *recognize* the actions that are leading to the harm.

Recognizing your detrimental behavior requires taking some time for self-observance. This is best done over a span that will give you a good cross section of your interactional process rhythm. A day may not expose everything, whereas a month may better reveal what the relational dance is like for the both of you. Once discovered, you can develop a game plan to change the harmful behavior.

Sometimes, it's easier to *substitute* harmful behavior than eliminate it. For example, give a direct compliment, rather than a backhanded one. Simply substituting better behavior can effectively alleviate harm to your relationship and it's a really effective way to say "I love you" to your companion.

42. Go

Not only do we need to stop some things that damage a relationship, but we sometimes need to *go* and get involved in things together that will enhance it. Go, and get your chores done. Go, and take responsibility for important matters. Go, and do an honest day's work. You get the picture.

It's very important to remain proactive in a relationship and taking responsibility to keep things in good shape. One of the common myths is that we get married, hope for the best, and it somehow works out. Frequently, when I do marriage counseling, the couple will say, "Divorce is not in our vocabulary". Obviously, it is, because they just used the word. What would make their relationship any different than the others?

What makes some relationships work while others don't? The scope of this entire book couldn't satisfactorily answer that question. One key observation, however, is that relationships tend to succeed when two companions intentionally work together to build a healthy style of relating. An *active* relationship tends to be most effective.

Simply sitting back and coasting is a relationship killer. Relationships die out in time, if left to themselves. Some people use their default setting of inertia, fail to take action, and neglect to feed the relationship. They need to become proactive. Doing chores around the house tells your companion that you are into the relationship. Initiating fun things together is also a real relationship builder. Taking responsibility and being proactive in the way you relate says "I love you."

43. Celebrate With Your Companion

Nothing quite conveys the notion of "I love you" like celebrating with your companion the things that he or she sees as important. When your companion achieves a promotion or gets that degree, celebrate to the fullest. Be their biggest fan. Support his or her dreams and be open to their ideas.

It's easy to overlook things that are important to your companion because you're around them every day. Important matters can get lost in the daily routines and hidden among the million things that must be done around the house. You may have been exposed to them for a long time and now you don't even notice anymore. Those things can slip right by you without notice.

Remain alert and celebrate with your companion when it's time. Celebrate both big accomplishments and small achievements. Rally when your companion reaches small goals or huge ones. Don't miss opportunities because you don't notice or don't remember.

One way to make sure you don't miss opportunities is to keep important matters on your calendar. Don't have one? Maybe it's time to figure out which type (paper or digital) will work best for you and develop a habit of working it every day. Place all important events, dates and reminders on the calendar, so you'll make time to celebrate and participate. If you don't work the calendar, opportunities will pass right by you. Don't leave it to your companion to remind you over and over. Log it in and do it.

44. Be Honest

Honesty is a fundamental building block of a healthy relationship. We can speak the truth in love, but it needs to be spoken. Honesty builds a foundation that will weather the storms that life brings. It builds security between two people that's not easily shaken and can withstand life's stressors and strains.

Neglecting to give *all* of the information is not truth. Not telling the truth to avoid conflict will drive a wedge between the two of you, leading to bigger problems and even more conflict. Some people deny something even while they're actively doing those very things. I've actually seen people deny that they did something, while watching a video clip of themselves in action. "That is not me!" they exclaimed. It was. How do you suppose the dishonesty impacted trust in their relationship?

How about you? Are you honest? To what degree? Can your word be trusted? Do you tell the truth or half truths? If you want to be trustworthy, tell and live the truth.

Lack of honesty has destroyed many relationships, but a habit of honesty builds a trusting and healthy one. Honesty allows you to deal with issues right up front. It also sends the message that you have confidence in your companion and believe in the two of you to work together and relate in a healthy way. It leads to a life of freedom with no cover-ups. You don't have to remember what you said to whom. You just tell the truth. Honesty is a great way to say "I love you"...and mean it!

45. Be Open

Openness is different than honesty. Openness is about *sharing yourself* with your companion. If you stay closed-off and withhold from your companion what's going on inside, then he or she is left to guess. That gets old after awhile.

I often hear people say, "I am a private person and don't like to talk." That behavior doesn't build a relationship. It usually brings distance instead of closeness. My favorite excuse for not being open: "I think it and, therefore, to say it would be redundant." You might have a few reasons of your own, but I would bet that they don't work any better than the aforementioned excuses.

After all, relationship is about sharing your life with another person. Are you really sharing your life when you don't open up? Relationship is about sharing life together—caring about each other's inner world. Having someone to care about you, your thoughts, your dreams and ideas cannot be bought with money. It's more valuable to have someone to share life's journey with than to have all the stuff in the world.

Openness requires risk and vulnerability. Unfortunately, we will sometimes get hurt in a relationship. It's nearly impossible to be in a long-term relationship without getting hurt from time-to-time. We usually don't mean to hurt the other person, but we sometimes do so nonetheless. There is risk in relationship, but openness is necessary for you to have a meaningful one. Being open with your companion will hugely state "I love you."

46. Kill Time Together

Life contains plenty of responsibility, but you also need to learn to kill time together. There is a right time to work and get things done, and there is also a time to just let it go. Sometimes, you need to sit down and do nearly nothing. At other times, you can do something fun and exciting together. Killing time could be going to a movie together or watching a sunset. Maybe you have a hobby that you both enjoy. Killing time together gives you the feel-good moment that goes in the plus column of your relationship.

Now think about the other side of this issue. If you can't let something go, it might say something about *you*. Are you taking life too seriously? Have you gotten so caught up in busyness that you won't let yourself relax? What hinders you from some much needed down-time? I'm not suggesting that you become irresponsible and fail to accomplish what's needed. Being responsible and getting things done will allow you to kick back without guilt. It might be difficult for you or your companion to relax if things are piled up. Being carefree is about enjoying the presence of your companion. Designating some down-time with them can enhance your relationship.

You'll also find that you can learn to wind down, even when you're working at something. If your style is to go full-force and knock chores out, you might get frustrated when things go wrong. You might benefit from slowing down some and enjoying the process a little. Kick back and lay it all down from time-to-time.

47. Listen

Listening has become a lost art. We have lots of monologue, but not much dialog. If you want to scream out (without words) "I LOVE YOU", then learn to listen to your companion. Listening is more than hearing the words; it is about grasping what the other person is trying to communicate. It's about valuing what your companion has to say—about placing value on his or her ideas. It has nothing to with agree or disagree; it's about hearing, understanding, perceiving, and grasping. It's about valuing the person as much as the ideas.

There are barriers to effective listening. Too often, we listen to evaluate (is what your companion saying accurate or inaccurate?). We listen to gather ammunition (using what they say against them or to make our point). We are distracted and don't actually listen at all. We don't even care enough to pay attention. We're thinking about what we need to say next or perhaps something else altogether.

Listening sends an important message to your companion that you *care* enough to pay attention. It sends a powerful message that you value him or her. You must truly care in order to listen. You can't fake it. It takes genuineness to set aside your thoughts long enough to focus on grasping what your companion is trying to communicate. Forget about agree/disagree for awhile and learn to truly listen, in order to understand your companion. You will discover that they have valuable contributions to the various topics of discussion. Say "I love you" to your companion by listening.

48. Laugh

Laughing together reduces stress and communicates well-being. After being together for awhile, people forget to laugh and have fun. They neglect small talk; it's small talk that reduces stress levels. As responsibility increases, it becomes easy to neglect taking time to enjoy yourselves. Laughing with your companion sends the message that you enjoy being with him or her.

There is a difference between laughing *at* someone and laughing *with* someone. Having fun at your companion's expense will only hurt them and, afterward, saying "I was only kidding" won't take that hurt away. Making your companion the butt-end of your jokes will damage your relationship.

In contrast, laughing *with* your companion will show your support. Life has some really light and funny moments. Enjoy them together. Learn to see the humor in life and share those moments together.

When couples get so bent out of shape on a regular basis, it can become hard to laugh and enjoy light moments. If you hold grudges you'll likely not be able to laugh and enjoy life very much. Sometimes forgiveness will be required for you to wipe the slate clean and allow yourselves to start over.

Proverbs tell us that laughter does good like a medicine. Do yourself and your companion a huge favor by laughing together. It will convey the idea that you love each other.

49. Set Aside The Agenda

In our minds, we have a template of how things should work or what should be. It makes perfect sense in our head. The agenda is usually unspoken. We just *know* that anyone with any common sense would think the same way. Why should it even come up, since this is the only "reasonable" thing to do? Two different agendas, his and hers, are common. Sometimes you will need to set aside your own agenda, in order to see the logic and benefits from the agenda of your companion. If not, you will only defend your own position and not even consider theirs.

Setting your agenda aside is not the same as always giving in and letting your companion have his or her way. It is simply taking a moment to grasp what your companion is trying to say. There will be time and methods to work out what's best. This is not to say that your ideas don't count; they do. If the two of you will learn to set aside your agenda long enough to listen and care, then it will position you both to find a course of action mutually acceptable.

Agendas drive us. They point us toward direction and motivate us into action. Give yourselves plenty of time to work through both of your agendas to make sure *all* needs and concerns are considered.

Become aware of both of your agendas. Learn to clearly communicate them and understand that of your companion. This practice will draw you closer together, as it's yet another way of saying "I love you."

50. Break Bread Together

There's nothing quite like eating together to cement a relationship. It's been known for decades that table time tends to provide fertile ground for relationship to flourish. Relaxed time over food tends to bring down stress levels and increase a sense of well-being. The topic of discussion is not nearly as important as the sense of caring about each other enough to listen, engage, and share. Besides, the topic or content will change continually, so just relax and enjoy the interaction.

Table time has become nonexistent or rushed in many homes today. Are you eating on-the-go or wolfing it down so you can get on to something else "more important"? Have you become a sink eater? You know, grabbing something and standing over the sink to slam it down and rinse away the evidence so you can get on with life. After awhile, life gets in the way and we don't take time to enjoy each other's presence over a meal.

One good way to invest in your relationship is to regularly have table time together. You'll have to *make* the time. You can do it at home or you can go out. Every week, we go to a neat little restaurant, close to where we live. We sit for a while to shut out the world and enjoy time with each other. It's a simple restaurant with simple food, good service and friendly staff. Sometimes, we spend a couple of hours there, relaxing from a long hard week and connecting with each other. Table time will energize your relationship and help you to remain friends. Make time to get together and relax over a meal.

51. Value What Your Companion Values

We live in a world that's self-focused. It's difficult to value what your companion values if you're self-focused. If you hope to value what your companion values, you'll need to set self aside for a little while. That doesn't mean that you don't count; it means that you can set yourself aside for the moment and think of someone else. If you see his or her ideas as unimportant or useless, you will not value what they value.

Valuing what your companion values means seeing him or her as a real person with important ideas. It's a state of mind or an attitude. Valuing what your companion values doesn't mean agreeing with them or giving up your ideas; yours are just as important and have their place too. It's fully acknowledging the person as valid and important.

The converse is just as true. If you fail to value what your companion values, you will send the message that he or she is not very important to you. You can't afford to excuse it away by saying that their sense of value is warped. You will discover that it's important to let your companion be who he or she really is.

There are reasons why people value certain things more than others, but getting to the *why* is not nearly as important as learning *what* your companion values. They may value time, things, friends, events, fun, security, peace, quiet time, excitement, etc. The list of what your companion values is endless and learning to share those values is an ongoing process for a lifetime. Stick with it and make it a habit. Sharing your companion's values is an important way of saying "I love you."

52. Pray For Your Companion

If you are given to spiritual matters, you can do a really big "I love you" by praying for your companion. There is nothing quite like knowing that your companion is praying for you. I was not aware of just how much this meant until several years ago. I was conducting a couple's retreat. During break time, as I was answering questions and chatting with people, a lady approached my wife who was standing very near me. Her question to my wife was: "I hear what your husband is teaching, but what is the one thing he does for you that means the most to you?" Now, to be frank with you, I don't remember what I was talking about with the person in front of me, as I was suddenly all ears for Linda's reply. She said the most important thing to her was "Don prays for me every day". Wow! Up until that point, I hadn't realized just how much that meant to her.

Praying will not necessarily solve all of the problems of this world, but it can connect you with God, who can help you through the problems. It can draw you and your companion closer together, give you some commonality, be a reminder that you are in this together and that God is leading you. You build unity and a sense that you're part of something bigger than you are. It helps you to keep perspective and discern between major and minor issues. What can sometimes look like major issues, when held up to the light of God, now seem minor. Prayer is a personal choice. However, it tells God that you love Him and your companion that you love him or her also.

Prayer is simply talking with God; so go ahead and chat with Him.

53. Develop A Hobby Together

Some couples naturally have common hobbies, while others do not. We often are attracted to, and marry one, who is very different from us. We don't always gravitate to the same hobbies and interests. I'm an outdoors guy and like things like fishing and all sorts of nature things. I can point out a really interesting moon alongside one of the planets. Linda will say "uh huh" and go right back to whatever she was doing. I'm all excited and she just takes a quick glance. I grab the telescope and she continues with her own interests. She totally supports what I like, but she has little interest in it for herself.

It is not necessary to do things that you really don't like doing. It's totally fine and healthy to have separate interests. What's nice, though, is when you're able to develop something you *can* do together. For example, we like going for a walk together, and it is even more fun if it's a beach we're walking on. We take day trips together and do some projects together. We also create artistic things and decorate the house together.

Some couples might have to work a little harder to discover things to do together that both will enjoy. Make it fun, like a treasure hunt, and you can discover things that will be enjoyable for the both of you, as well as a rewarding way to spend time together. It'll be well worth the effort you put into it and draw you closer together as a couple. I would also add that keeping an open mind will help you get there quicker.

Spending time together doing something that you both enjoy will say "I love you" in a unique way.

54. Shut Off Your Phone

Ouch! I know, I know, you don't let your phone get in the way; you don't do all that much on it. If I had a dime for every time I heard that.... Electronics have intruded into many relationships. It is not just the phone, but the TV, the computer, the gaming device, etc. Some families can't even enjoy a meal without the phone. People even sleep with one. While electronics are really handy, helpful, and even fun, they can intrude into relationships. People enter a restaurant, sit down for a meal and out come the phones. Conversation and connection with each other have taken a back seat.

How about you? Are you letting electronics get between you and your companion? How much are electronics intruding upon your important relationships? Take an honest and realistic inventory. If they aren't, then a huge congratulations to you! But if they are, it might be time to rethink how you want to use electronics.

I suggest that you not take the easy way out, quickly negating the issue without much thought and telling yourself that it's not a problem for you. Study the matter thoroughly before putting it to rest. Observe yourself for awhile to see just how much you unknowingly inject electronics into your relationship. If you need to make changes, develop a plan. Dealing with electronics in blocks of time can keep you from watering down the time you have with the people you love.

Shifting electronics out from between you and your companion can be a huge "I love you."

55. Surprise Your Companion

Surprises can be fun. They can range from little things to a huge trip or gift. Even a cold glass of tea on a hot day can be a really cool surprise. You don't have to break the bank to surprise your companion. Think about the little things that he or she likes and just do them. Both my wife and daughter are really good at this one. They're both thoughtful and notice things that would go right over my head. They got together and bought a really nice telescope for my birthday. They seem to come up with ideas that I never would have thought of.

To make it a pleasant surprise, you'll need to really know your companion. If not, you'll likely do what *you* would like instead. It has to be focused on the other person and not about you. You'll also need to be aware of how it will play out. If you surprise your companion with a trip and he or she is not the type to go on a moment's notice, you might be stuck at home. Maybe they just can't transition that fast. Make sure you know your audience.

Good surprises communicate that you're thinking about your companion and not yourself. If you have the staff at the restaurant to come out clapping and singing happy birthday, but your companion is shy and doesn't like attention, the surprise will not likely go in the plus column. He or she might smile on the outside, but it may mask a different sentiment on the inside, such as "you don't really know me do you?" The key to a good surprise is that it hits the spot with the receiver.

56. Take Fun Pictures

One year in the fall, we did two day trips to the Blue Ridge Parkway, taking over two hundred photos of the changing colors of the leaves. We've gone to the falls on the parkway and to the beach. We have a collection of pictures from coast-to-coast and have enjoyed the experiences. Part of the fun is taking the pictures and part is the experience of being there. One of the funniest shots was when both my wife and daughter were fighting gnats as I was telling them to stand still. They were swatting like crazy. There must have been a million gnats and that's no exaggeration. It made a great shot and captured a funny moment. Sometimes the fun ones are the best.

With digital cameras, you can take unlimited pictures and decide later which ones you want to keep. It also allows you to risk shots you couldn't afford with film. You can take a ton of them with no risk or expense, unless you decide to print them. Digital storage has become fast and easy. It's easy to have a camera or phone handy at all times and take pictures as opportunities arise.

Part of the enjoyment of taking pictures is the experience that you're reveling in at the time. Your pictures preserve memories and take you back in time, allowing you to re-experience the occasion all over again. Fun pictures stand for all time and keep the memories of the relationship alive and vibrant.

It's easy to take pictures, so get out and have some fun. Make some memories. You'll discover that taking fun pictures together will connect you as a couple and convey the notion of "I love you."

57. Feed The Pets

Sometimes it is cruel how people treat pets. They don't want to bother with it or don't have time. Caring for your pets sends a strong message about your humanity. If you don't take care of your pets, there is a fairly strong indicator that you might not care about the well being of people. A few years ago, a movie depicted recovering addicts that were told to get a plant and care for it. They were told when they could care for a plant, they might be able to have a relationship.

How you treat pets and living things can reflect how you see relationships. If you can care about living things, you can care for and attend a relationship.

Feeding the pet might reflect how you care for your companion. It is about participating around the house. It is about caring about what your companion thinks is important. You are communicating that you care when you feed the pet, water the flower, or take out the trash.

You will need to *notice* what needs to be done if you desire to convey the message that you care. If you must be told what to do, you will send a strong message that you really do not care, but are only doing it because you were asked. It is wise to develop a habit of noticing and doing before being asked. Do it because it needs to be done.

The way you care for pets will color how your companion views you. Are you attentive or fail to notice what needs to be done? Caring for her cat or his dog will send a powerful message of "I love you". He or she will notice that you care.

58. Try Something New Together

Linda and I try many new things together. We've gone to places that we've never gone before and we're currently making plans to do a different sort of vacation than we have experienced before. It can be something simpler, however. We recently played a new game with a couple. You can try a new food or some different décor. I have friends that are doing dance lessons and other friends getting into martial arts. I know a couple who got a massage together and loved the experience. Some couples have gotten a gym membership; others joined a choir. Use your imagination to think of something that you would love to try. Take the adventure together. It is more fun when you have someone you love to share the experience.

Make sure that these new adventures are something both of you might enjoy. Don't manipulate your companion into the things you like and have always dreamed about, with little or no regard for what he or she likes to do.

It takes time and effort to begin something new together. Some adventures take planning, and you might need to study the situation before embarking on something new. Invest time in researching what's involved and required to be successful. It's normally not wise to jump into something new without doing your homework first.

Trying something new together will keep your relationship alive and vibrant. It's easy to get bored when you do the same old things over and over, but new experiences keep the energy going and bring excitement. Who better to try something new with than you own companion?

59. Remember People Who Are Special To Your Companion

Your companion has friends and important people in his or her life. When you value them or remember them you're honoring your companion. Conversely, if you make fun of or criticize their friends and important people, you dishonor your companion. Criticizing or putting down your companion's friends will not sit well with them.

It's a fact that people don't always choose the best of friends, but that doesn't mean you should run them down. It's wise to choose wholesome friends and make good choices. You don't need to be best friends with your companion's best friend, but you do need to realize that it's your companion's friend.

Whenever you can, it's wise to remember the people that are important to your companion and sharing interest in them. That could be as simple as following up to see how his or her day went while with a friend.

Each person in a relationship needs to have friends of his or her own. It is good to have mutual friends, but people also need to have friends that are theirs alone. For example, I have fishing partners and guys that share my interest in hobbies that I enjoy— ones in which Linda has no interest. Likewise, she has her own set of friends who enjoy her interests.

It's wise to be grateful for the people in the life of your companion. They are important to your companion and should be important to you. Make a genuine effort to remember the people that are special to your companion.

60. Provide A Romantic Atmosphere

It would be nice, once, in a while, to set the stage for a romantic evening. That could be a simple thing like lowering the lighting, or it might be more involved like creating an entire romantic atmosphere. Of course, you could have someone provide it for you, such as going to a romantic restaurant where the atmosphere is already set. You have many options.

For some it's easy, but for those of us who are not romantically inclined, it's more of a stretch. However, it doesn't have to be complicated. A flower, a candle and some soft music during a meal can change the atmosphere entirely. Think about what might be romantic to your companion.

Check your motivation first. If your goal is to "get" something, the evening will not likely go over nearly as well as you'd like it to. Your motive will show through. If your child, suddenly out of the blue, offers to do the dishes because he thinks it will help him get that new video game, your first thought is going to be a suspicious one—"what does he want?" Your own motives will be just as obvious if they are self-serving ones. Make sure you're providing a romantic atmosphere *for your companion* and not for yourself. It's all about doing something nice for your companion and thinking about them instead of yourself.

Providing for a romantic evening tells your companion that you care and enjoy being with him or her. It conveys the message that you've paid attention enough to know what they like and are willing to provide it. It's a great way to say "I love you."

61. Take Care Of The Car

A car is a huge investment, or should I say expenditure. You spend a pile of money on it. Taking care of it sends a message that you care about your financial well being. Change the oil, clean it up and keep it well maintained. It will give you more bang for your buck if you do.

For some people, it's also about image. Driving a dirty car is difficult for some people. Washing her car says I love you and I'm thinking about you. Washing the car communicates that you are aware of her needs and are willing to meet those needs.

Picking up the french fries from the floor of the car says you respect your investment. Since a car is such a huge expenditure, it's wise to make it last and keep it in good shape. Keeping your car well serviced will protect your investment. It also conveys the idea that you care.

It goes way beyond the car. If you leave the tools out in the rain to rust, who would want to buy new ones for you? If you waste the resources you have, who wants to provide more? Look around and notice what you respect and care for. Notice what you take for granted, waste, or fail to take care of.

Taking care of the car or other things you have will send a strong message that you care. Washing her car will convey the message that you are thinking about her and want what is best for her. It may not yield a new tool set for you, but it surely will go in the plus column.

62. Allow The Conversation To Meander

Some conversations have a specific purpose and should be attended carefully. Others sometimes need to be allowed to meander about, taking you where they will. It's not all business in life, so stop and smell the roses. You can't do that if you don't meander a little. Animals communicate, but we humans have a higher form of exchanging messages that can take us to all sorts of moods, destinations, decisions, etc.

All forms of communication are important and have their place. There is a time to get serious and settle a matter; there is a time to explore, in order to survey the possibilities; there is a time to brainstorm; there is a time for straight talk; and then there is a time to let the conversation meander about and flow freely.

Meandering communicates that you are comfortable with your companion, like being with him or her, and not always in pursuit of an agenda. When you relax enough to allow the conversation to meander, you're honoring each other and putting trust in one another. It creates an atmosphere of its own.

Meandering includes free-flowing conversation and casual listening. There's not much evaluation going on and there are few agree/disagree moments. Meandering conversation is not nearly as focused as other types and it's largely informal. When you're allowing yourselves to meander in conversation, you're enjoying the engagement and fellowship of your companion. The experience is more important than the topic.

63. Go Visit Someone Together

There is something to be said about reaching out to or doing something for someone else. Sure it eats up some of your time to go visit someone, but it is more like an investment. Linda and I have visited people in just about every circumstance—at the birth of a baby, the loss of a family member, a wedding, a stay in the hospital, an open house or just for the fun of it. Getting together with others can bring life to your relationship. Fellowship can be rewarding and enriching.

Helping someone is even better. Linda shoveled snow from our neighbor's walk and that neighbor still remembers her kindness, bringing it up periodically. Reaching out to someone taps into the caring place inside you and keeps you a little more sensitive to the needs of others. If you never reach out to others, you might take an inventory to see if you need to develop a caring spirit. It will bleed over to your companion as well.

It's important that you have friends as a couple. We don't go it alone in life; we need friends along the way. Friends add spice to life. Having friends helps us remember that relationship is a couple's journey and not just a solo flight. You're in this together.

At first glance, visiting someone together appears to be totally for the other person; in reality, however, it will enrich your relationship as well. Investing in the lives of others is surely helpful to them and it also goes in the plus column in your own relationship. It's healthy for your companion to see you invest in the lives of others.

64. Share Something You Have Learned

There is so much to be learned in this world. You'll do yourself a huge favor if you stay in the learning mode; you'll be boring if you don't. But don't keep it to yourself; share it. And who better to share it with than your companion. You don't have to become a know-it-all or bore your companion to tears, but sharing something exciting that you've learned is a relationship builder.

Celebrate and appreciate something your companion has learned. Even if it's something you already know, you can still appreciate that it's something your companion has learned. Be interested in the growth of your mate, and it will tell him or her that you care. Make growth orientation the norm in your relationship. It helps to read books about relationship and learn things together. That alone can be an exciting adventure.

Learning begins with a right attitude. You have to *want* to learn. If you keep an open mind, there will be millions of bits of information that you'll acquire. There are so many interesting things to learn in the course of a lifetime. It's fun to share with your companion the things you've learned. It doesn't have to be something huge or rocket science; just share the little things.

Sharing these things provides small talk that greases the gears of the relationship. If you only share things you've learned with others, and not with your companion, then he or she will feel left out. Small talk goes a long way in keeping stress levels down in a relationship. Go ahead and share a new discovery with your companion. Make it a good habit.

65. Dinner And A Movie

This is an old stand-by that never seems to go out of date. The real genius behind this is to have dedicated time that you'll spend together. Movies are at set times, so you have to plan at least a little. It's something you can look forward to doing together. It's not necessarily the dinner or the movie, as much as it is the designated time together.

Seems like everything in the world will swoop in to take the time that you could spend together. Dinner and a movie somehow overrides that. There are other things that you can do to have designated time together, if you get intentional and make the time to do so. Make your own list of things the two of you could do together that requires a little planning and dedicated time.

When you go for dinner and a movie, you'll be able to have leisure time together. You can talk and enjoy each other. The movie provides entertainment of some sort, so you don't have to be a total romantic to have a successful evening. You might get to laugh a little and maybe even cry a little. At the very least, you'll be able to enjoy something together.

Dinner and a move is a proven way to have regular time together as a couple. Fortunately, there are enough new movies to keep you from getting bored. You can plan as many as you like and it will afford enough time together on a regular basis to keep you connected. The key is to find ways to have the time together to regularly connect so that the relationship will not stagnate. Dinner and a movie is one way of getting that time together.

66. Plant Something Together

I know a couple that plants a tree together every year. It's not a huge deal, but they do it regularly. Sometimes it's in honor of something or someone, but at other times, they just do it because they want to. And it makes a difference in the environment. It's not something that breaks the bank for them, but is something that will make a lasting difference. You could plant a shrub or a flower together. You could pot a plant or grow a garden. One year, we planted a bonsai. It actually lived a few years, but we finally figured out how to kill it.

Working in the dirt can give you a sense of well-being and lift your mood. There's something about getting in the dirt that seems to elevate your spirits. The physical activity is helpful, but the connection with nature cannot be underestimated.

Planting something together connects us with each other as well. When you plant flowers and shrubs around the house, you're beautifying the property. People take joy in planting a garden together and receive huge benefits from vegetables and melons.

Planting something together also makes an impact on the environment. It's a simple way for the two of you to contribute to the overall good of humanity. It may not feel like a big deal, but each plant makes a difference. You may not see the big picture, but you can enjoy your time together and, in some small way, make a difference at the same time. Go ahead, plant something together and have a little fun as you are doing so.

67. Kiss

What a way to start and end a day! A kiss makes a really bold statement of "I love you!" There are different kinds of kisses, but all of them usually convey the notion of love and affection. At our house, we kiss before either of us leave in the morning, and we kiss when we get home in the evening. It's a fantastic way to say hello and goodbye. For some reason, kissing never gets old and never loses its meaning.

Do you remember kissing when you first met? Kissing is a natural part of growing close together. The sad part is that, over the years, people get out of the habit of kissing. They let it slide. For some couples, it's been years since they've kissed. It's easy, in a busy world, to just "forget".

Anger is a kiss killer! It's a little difficult to kiss when you're agitated with each other. This is another good reason to keep your relationship in good shape. Many of the things we enjoy so much at the beginning of the relationship get shoved to the side when irritability takes over. Work on your relationship so it will grow strong and healthy and keep the kiss alive and well.

Giving a kiss out of obligation will be spotted a mile away, but sincere kisses will carry warm meaning. I would rather my wife know, as we depart for the day, that I'm in love with her. It then gives me the opportunity to start the evening sending a message that I'm *still* in love with her. And, of course, you can sneak one in from time-to-time just for the fun of it. Go ahead, give a kiss and let it say "I love you."

68. Get Away From It All

There are many ways to get away from it all. You can go out of town on a vacation for several days; you can take a day trip; you can turn off the phone for a day and just be together; you can do something exciting like a theme park or the zoo; you can go to the park for a picnic. There are endless things you can do to unplug and get away from the rat race of life.

Think of things you might enjoy doing together. We've taken a day trip to the beach; browsed a favorite store together; driven the Blue Ridge Parkway; gone to quaint little spots that have no cell phone service; and just gone for a leisurely drive. Find ways to unplug and have some time together so that you're not pulled in all directions by your job or other busy matters. Those things are important, but there is a time to get away from it all and just enjoy each other.

Getting away from it all will help you recharge you batteries, encourage closeness with each other, and build energy for you to face the responsibilities of life. It will help you remember the importance of relationship and make time for it. You might not be able to get away for a whole day, but you could put down the phone for dinner. You might not be able to get out of town for a vacation this week, but the two of you could go out to dinner.

Think in blocks of time, when it comes to getting away from it all. You might not be able to do all you want, but do what you can. Make a regular practice of getting away from it all and enjoy some renewal time.

69. Be A Gentleman/Be A Lady

Most of us enjoy being with a lady or gentleman. Be a gentleman by getting the door and using good manners. Saying "thank you" is still in style. Have some dignity, respect and honor. Be the person of integrity that your companion will want to be around. Be a lady that doesn't have to have drama going all the time. And be one in both attitude and lifestyle.

I'm not referring to going back to the Victorian era. I'm referring to how you fundamentally conduct yourself. Anyone can be a gentleman or lady. It doesn't require money or status; it requires the right attitude. It's about how you treat people and conduct yourself.

Thinking about others is a good starting place, if you want to be a gentleman or lady. Set your own thoughts and preferences aside long enough to see what others need and tend to those needs, rather than your own. If you're self-absorbed, you'll not notice what others need. You'll also likely encroach on the space of others.

At a wedding, I once saw some guys who were drinking to the point that they became loud and obnoxious—the center of attention. They were ruining the evening for the wedding party. I doubt that anyone in attendance would have labeled them "gentlemen". Gentlemen wouldn't have thought of themselves first; they would have been considerate of the wedding party.

It's rather simple, but not always easy, to be a gentleman or lady. You simply need to be aware of the big picture and do your part. Just a little thoughtfulness will go a long way in becoming one.

70. Relax Together

There are tons of projects that need to be done and the towels will need to be laundered again tomorrow. The work will never really be finished, because very soon after you've completed the tasks, they'll need to be done all over again. It is important that you get the work done. If not, you won't have the peace-of-mind that allows you to truly relax.

Make time to relax together. It's okay to take five and relax. Grab a glass of tea and just visit for a few minutes. There is a time to work and a time to relax.

Working hard is good for you, but so is relaxation. Relaxation gives an opportunity to catch up and take another look at things. When you are so caught up in the rat race that you forget to relax, life can become all work and no play. So, mix it up a little, throw in some relaxation and enjoy each other's presence.

Relaxation comes in many forms, from sitting on the deck together and watching the hummingbirds to having a cup of coffee and chatting. It could be taking the time to smell the fresh cut grass and enjoy all the hard work you've invested in the lawn together. It might be a cool dip in the pool on a hot day or a card or board game that the two of you enjoy.

The setting is not nearly as important as the attitude. You'll need to set aside all else, so you're not worrying about the to-do list. Relaxation is all about enjoying the moment and letting go of everything else for a little while. Relaxing together will not complete your check list, but it will convey a huge "I love you."

71. Serve Each Other

I hope you've noticed by now that a healthy relationship is more about what you do than what you get. Our selfish nature focuses too much on what we *get* and too little on what we *give*. We need to learn to turn that equation around. If you take more than you give, you'll end up with a deficit in your relationship. It will end up in the red, just as too many bank accounts do.

Look for opportunities to serve each other. There are, perhaps, millions of ways to serve your companion, so pay attention and you'll learn to see them. It will require you to look for opportunities and seize the moment. My wife doesn't merely get one bath towel; she gets out two, so I'll have one to use. That's service! See how practical serving can be? When you get tea for yourself, how about getting some for your companion? Pour that extra cup of coffee for him or her.

Sometimes service is not so easy or glamorous. When someone is sick, it's more of a challenge to clean up after them than it is to pour that extra cup of coffee. It's as important to serve in difficult times and situations as it is in the easy times. Sometimes service is inconvenient, but it's worth it. Serving each other costs time, energy and sometimes money. It's about giving willfully because you want to. It's about learning to notice the needs of your companion and taking joy in fulfilling those needs. Serving tells your companion that you care and are thinking about him or her. It will never be wasted time or effort.

72. Leave A Voice Message

We live in a time when we're expected to be available 24/7, so for some people, not answering the phone has become a negative message. Somehow, that concept has gotten twisted. I regularly see people fight over that issue. How about turning the voicemail into a positive experience? How do you think your companion would feel if, when there is no answer, you simply left a warm "thinking about you" message? I like something quick and warm like: "Hey babe, just thinking about you— hope you're having a good day. I can't wait to see you. I love you babe. See you soon." Yep, go ahead and wipe off the sap and think about that for a moment. How do you think she feels when she hears that message? I'm guessing that she looks forward to seeing me in the evening, when she gets home. Unfortunately, the most common things I hear from people go more like this: "Where are you?", "You never answer the phone!", "Why don't you answer the stupid phone?", "Call me back!" or "You don't care about your family enough to answer the _____ phone!" If you leave a message like that, do you really think your companion will be looking forward to coming home?

Realize that you do have a choice. You can be proactive, thoughtful and leave a message that will have a positive impact. Or you can let your emotions wash over you, react, and shoot yourself in the proverbial foot. It's your choice. A quick and easy way to say "I love you" is to leave a brief thoughtful and warm message for your companion. Give it a try sometime. Leave a message that communicates love and affection.

73. Don't Continually Check To See If Your Companion Still Loves You.

Sometimes there's an internal mechanism that produces the urge to "check and see" if our companion still loves us. Insecurity can drive us to continually check. Don't give into that urge. Your companion loves you, but can't quite get that message to stick and must prove, over and over, that he or she still loves you. Imagine being on the receiving end, with your companion continually checking with you. Think how frustrating that would be.

Love is often measured by little things and, if you're not attentive, you'll negate the very ways your companion is trying to convey love to you. You see what you want to see and discount what you think is unimportant or not meaningful to you. Be careful that you're not blind to the ways your companion is trying to convey a loving message to you. Notice what your companion *is* doing to say "I love you." If you have your companion jumping through all sorts of hoops that you prefer, it might quickly get old to him or her. In reality, we *do* need for our companion to consistently convey love to us. Having them prove it by jumping through our specific—and sometimes unstated—hoops quite often backfires.

Saying "I love you" is extremely important and each of us need to hear it on a regular basis. However, constantly having your companion under pressure to prove it, over and over, will eventually push him or her away. Allowing it to happen is much better than the constant pressure to make it happen.

74. Dream Together

Dreaming together takes time. You'll probably not dream together on the fly. Instead, you'll need to create some down time. It happens best when there's no agenda. Dreaming together is a sharing of ideas that may or may not go anywhere. Hold off on the evaluation of ideas and let them flow. Letting unchecked and unevaluated ideas flow can be really fun and a few may even be worth pursuing. Let yourself imagine things for the future or for a project. Let the ideas tumble out without judgment.

A sure-fire way to prohibit dreaming together is to evaluate. This will stop the dreaming process cold. As soon as you deem ideas "good" or "bad", the dreaming stops. It's tempting to evaluate each idea as it comes out, but resist that temptation. Use self control and don't let that happen.

Dreaming together has several positive outcomes. I'll focus on just two here. First, it helps us achieve things that are important to us, using two heads instead of one. Second, we move closer as a couple when we achieve something together. Honoring each other enough to consider thoughts and ideas as valuable and find ways to work together build relationships.

Dreaming together usually occurs as you have some regular down time and just let it happen, rather than setting a time to do so. Imagine that you set up an hour to dream. Odds are that it probably wouldn't happen in that allotted time period. However, when you have regular, relaxed down time, you have fertile ground for it to occur. Just let go and dream.

75. Talk It Out

No, I don't mean fight it out; I mean talk it out. Have you realized that fighting is not very helpful? I regularly hear the statement that you need to "fight fair". Really? Do you really need to fight at all? Let's see how that sounds in a statement: "My companion and I really need to have a good, fair fight about once a month!" How does that sound to you?

I guess I must be a lover, not a fighter. I haven't seen one time when a fight brought us closer together at our house. But I suppose that, if you feel that fights really bring you and your companion closer together, then you ought to skip to the next page.

Talking things out can actually honor both of you. Taking enough time to really listen to your companion, trying to understand and value what he or she is experiencing and saying, will bring you closer together. You'll also need to value yourself enough to disclose what's inside you and convey those thoughts as clearly as you can. Sometimes, we don't say what we mean or don't understand what our companion is trying to say. Stop and clarify.

Embrace each other enough to value one another's experiences and ideas. Valuing requires us to treat each other with respect and honor. However, it doesn't require *agreement*. Patiently working with your companion can help you learn to talk it out. And you can do so with just about anything, if you're willing to slow down and value each other. This can bring you closer together as a couple.

76. Accept Your Companion For Who He Or She Is

The most fun topic I've taught over the years is about personality styles. Personality style is about clusters of characteristics and studying them gives a deep respect for each person and values each person for who he or she is. I find that learning about people helps us appreciate them even more. Some are more social and really like being with lots of people, drawing energy from them. Others are given to details and are really good with quality control and research. Some are good at getting a task done, while others are warm and nurturing.

A powerful way to say "I love you" is to accept your companion's personality as part of who he or she is. We're often drawn to someone who's different than we are. While we like some of the same things and finish each other's sentences, most of us pair up with someone who's different from us. What a boring world it would be if we were all the same. Different is good. I'm all about big picture and Linda is detail oriented. Together, we make a good team, but individually we have gaps in our qualities.

Learn to see your companion for all he or she brings to the relationship. If you focus on what you *don't* like about them, you'll miss a host of good qualities. I've come to appreciate that Linda does things right the first time. She's taught me that if I don't have time to do things right the first time, when will I find time to do them over? In the process, I've also learned that slowing things down can actually get you there faster. Learn to accept your companion for who he or she is and you just might learn something about yourself, as well.

77. Learn Self Control

We learn some self control as we grow up, but not nearly enough. Even after arriving into adulthood, we still have a good bit of maturity to achieve. Self control is learned and not just something we're necessarily born with. You can develop it. You have the power to do this, but you'll need to have the "want to", in order to achieve it. It starts in the heart. If you just want your way or think you know best, then self control will not be in your arsenal. You have to want it and you'll have to work at it. You can't just think it into place.

Developing self control isn't easy, but it is achievable. One of the first steps is to change how you think about it. Let's say that someone gets onto you about something. You could immediately snap back in defense. This, of course, wouldn't require much self control at all. However, you have another option. You could stop, think, and realize that this person is upset about something and then take the time to find out what that is. By showing a little grace during those times, rather than snapping back, you might discover that it's something that could be worked out between you. It may also not even be about *you* at all. Maybe this person is just having a bad day. We all occasionally have those.

Slowing down to think can help you develop self control, and as a result, you might have less drama in your relationship. You have the choice of getting lathered up about something or developing self control. Self control can powerfully communicate the notion of "I love you".

78. Think Forward

Thinking forward is simply thinking ahead. It's about seeing what will happen when we take action or make choices. It's anticipating the consequences of our actions and, therefore, requires us to resist the pressure of the moment.

Thinking forward best occurs when you step back and take a moment to think through an issue. You'll be wise to give your brain time to consider options other than the first one that comes to mind. Thinking forward considers the consequences of each option.

Thinking forward will prevent a huge amount of grief and turmoil in your relationship. You can avoid the typical pitfalls if you will learn to think forward. Stop long enough to think through the options and figure out how actions might play out. What will happen if you say what comes to mind? Will it go in the plus column or the minus column? How about if you buy that new fishing rod and reel— will it go in the plus or the minus column?

It takes self discipline to think forward. It's just the opposite of shooting from the hip. Slow down, take time to think of various options, consider the consequences of those options (both pros and cons) and make wise choices.

Your companion will thank you for dong the hard and tedious work of thinking forward. It's not easy or convenient to do it; it's painstaking work. But it's well worth the effort.

79. Give The Look

You probably have heard of "the look". No doubt, you've probably been on the receiving end of one when you've done something wrong or are suspect. Oooooooh, that negative look is so intense and chock-full of emotion and meaning. Sometimes, we feel like "the look" could kill us. This is not the look that you want to give. There's another kind.

Pay attention to people who are at the beginning development of their relationship. They look each other in the eyes and send all sorts of messages of fondness. How long has it been since you've given your companion the look that says "I love you"? Do you look at him or her with fondness and warmth or do you have the look of contempt? Your eyes will reveal what's truly in your heart, so your fondness for your companion must be genuine, lest they see something entirely different.

We forget about the look that we have. We forget that looks can both kill and convey warmth. You can spot it all the way across the room. Take time to become aware of the look that you cast. Could someone say that yours is a look that kills? Do they routinely say that you care? Do you have that "deer in the headlights" look? Pay attention to the message you send with "the look".

If you really want to say "I love you" with the look, start by making sure that your heart is right toward your companion. Keep it free of bitterness with forgiveness and by dealing with things as they come up. Letting go of offenses can help to keep your heart pure and allow you to intentionally say "I love you" with *the look*.

80. Do Good Self Care

Nothing says "I love you" quite like good self care. It might sound selfish, but in reality it's just the opposite. If you don't value yourself, you'll not likely value your companion.

One of my favorite stories is about what happens on a commercial airplane when we're preparing for takeoff. The flight attendant shows how to fasten and unfasten the seat belt, use the seat cushion for a floatation device and how to use the oxygen mask, if the cabin should lose pressure. But the best part comes next. They tell you that if you're traveling with small children, to put *your* mask on first, then assist your children with theirs. There is not a mother on the plane that will do that. It feels too selfish to put herself before her children for anything. Of course, there's a good reason why they tell you this. If you don't get your own functioning first, you may not have enough oxygen to assist your kids; then you'll all be in trouble. Another good reason for this is that people freak out during difficulty and simply putting your mask on first will *model* for your kids; then you can assist them in doing so.

Self care is, in fact, showing concern for others by taking care of you. It can be really frustrating to your companion when you don't do good self care. People sometimes get married and stop giving a second thought about self care. Good self care is not selfish, but thoughtful. Taking care of your own well-being will relieve tension for your companion, as he or she sees that you are keeping yourself in good shape. Learn to keep yourself in good shape by doing consistent self care.

81. Manage Your Emotions

All of us have emotions. Emotions, themselves, are neither good nor bad; they just are. The key is to *manage* them. We don't want to stifle our emotions, but we do need to learn to control what we do with them.

Emotions are the spice of life. Think what life would be if we didn't have emotions. We'd be like robots, unable to love. What really counts is that we don't let emotions rule us. They can hijack us. They can lead us astray or they can tell us what's important. Think about how you might feel if one of your family members were in harm's way and you didn't know their condition or whereabouts. You'd have that certain feeling in the pit of your stomach, until you were assured that they were safe and sound.

Emotions are like road signs—they tell us what's there. We don't have to act on them, but we're wise to notice what they tell us. Seeing a sign for your favorite restaurant, while driving down the road, doesn't mean that you have to stop and eat there. You have the choice of driving on. Emotions are like that. They tell you what's there, but they don't dictate what you *must* do.

One thing you can do to send a strong message of "I love you" to your companion is to learn to manage your emotions. If your emotions get out of hand, your companion could actually be afraid of you or learn to not trust you. By managing your emotions, you provide a safe and secure atmosphere that's pleasant to be in. This atmosphere will be one where love can be freely given and freely received.

82. Allow For Flexibility

Routine is a good thing, but flexibility is just as important. There's a tension between stability (keeping things the same) and change. There needs to be enough stability to make life function well and to have enough predictability so that people know what to count on. We also need to have flexibility so that life doesn't get one-sided and stuck in a rut.

Companionship requires that we don't have our way all of the time and that we learn to accommodate each other. We have different ideas about everything from where we should vacation to how to plant flowers. The template in our mind tells us there's one right way to do it and we often think that any thinking person would do it that way. However, there are many ways to achieve things.

Flexibility sends a message that you think your companion has a brain in his or her head. If you're not flexible, you send just the opposite message and treat your companion like they couldn't possibly have a good idea. That would be a really bad put-down. Do you really want to send that message?

Flexibility is more of an attitude than an event. It's not the same thing as compromise, nor is it negotiation. It's seeing that there are more options than one. It's learning to consider other ideas as reasonable. Flexibility considers the other person, as well as self. When you learn to be flexible, you're sending a strong message that you believe in your companion. One way to learn flexibility is to slow down, step back and see a bigger picture. You see much more with a panoramic view than with a narrow one.

83. Step Back And Think

We so often get caught up in what's right in front of us that we fail to see the big picture. Stepping back and taking it in will go a long way in communicating "I love you" to your companion. If you learn to see things from a panoramic view, you'll more effectively see what's going on.

However, if you pounce on the first thing you see, you'll likely miss some important information. Learn to see a bigger picture. What information are you missing? Will the thing that is upsetting you at the moment make a huge difference in a year from now? Is the sky really falling? Often, when we step back and think, things might look differently.

A common problem in communication is that we see what we want to see or we have tunnel vision. Feelings get in the way, we get swept up in the moment and our attention is drawn to what *feels* important. We *notice* pieces of information that confirm what we feel and from this compilation of material, we build our case. The major problem this creates is that the information is usually incomplete; it's skewed toward our tunnel vision. There's usually more than one side to the issue.

One of the best ways to address that problem is to pause, take a step back and think. Thinking things through will put them in a new light. If you will allow for a little objectivity, you might be able to fill in the gaps of your thinking and develop a fuller picture. Learn to think before you speak and act. This is a great way to say "I love you" and see more broadly than before.

84. Get'R Done

Have you ever left a scrap of paper on the counter instead of putting it in the trash can? Have you left your mug on the coffee table for your companion to pick up? Have you promised to pay the water bill, only to let it become overdue until they threaten to shut off the water? Have you promised for the past year to fix the leaky faucet? Collect your own list and ask yourself a question: "Do these things bring you two closer together?" Didn't think so. They don't for the rest of us either.

There's a long list of things that you just need to get done. You don't need to think about it for months; you need to just do it. Learn to pick up after yourself, take care of your responsibilities, etc. Just "get'r done". Make a habit of doing things when they need to be done.

My wife is probably the best example that I know of for getting things done, without question. She sees a need, jumps on it and keeps things done as they come up. She doesn't let them slide until tomorrow; she deals with them now. She never lets things pile up. Keeping things done as you go is a much more peaceful way to live.

If you pause, you'll think of all sorts of excuses to put things off. Oh, I'll do it later; I'm too tired right now; I don't have time now to fool with it; it will be there when I get back or it's not that big of a deal. Add your favorites to the list. Excuses lead to procrastination. You can strip a lot of irritation out of the relationship by getting things done. The best way to achieve this is to deal with things the moment you see them. Just get'r done!

85. Give Trust

It's a great feeling to come home to trust and not meet the look of "where were you, *really*?" It's peaceful when your companion doesn't go through your things with suspicion and question or feeling that you must weigh every word carefully before speaking. It's a wonderful feeling to know that you're trusted because of who you are—for your character.

How about giving the gift of trust to your companion? Trusting him or her will bond the two of you and provide fertile soil for warmth and intimacy. If your companion must walk on pins and needles because you don't trust them, there will be guardedness. They won't be able to relax in your presence because they'll be in a continual state of alertness. You'll notice that they'll relax with friends and have a good time with them, but not with you. Giving trust will allow your companion to relax with you and bring out the best. It conveys the message that you believe in your companion.

However, if your companion is not trustworthy, is unfaithful, will not tell the truth or hides things, it will be difficult to give trust. You might need to deal with those matters. Be wise in how you approach the topic; use a loving, direct approach. If you can't resolve matters by yourselves, you may want to seek council to remedy the situation. It's important that you don't impose your trust issues from past relationships onto your companion. Give trust whenever you can.

86. Be Trustworthy

A fundamental building block of a relationship is trust. A sure-fire way to destroy a relationship is to kill trust. Are you who you say you are? Are you the same with your family as you are in public? Are you honest? Can people depend on you? Do you forget things, hide things, cover up or tell partial truths? Do you have habits or behaviors that, if discovered, would leave a question mark? If what you do in secret came to light, would anyone question it? Do you have eyes for him or her only? How trustworthy are you? Do you make it difficult for your companion to trust you?

Trustworthiness is one of the greatest gifts you can give to your companion. They'll never have to check up on you and it will take the suspicion right out of the picture. There is nothing quite like being with someone you can trust completely. We live in a day when a person's word doesn't mean much. When I was young, my dad would make a deal and stick to his word without question. He was a man of his word and one of integrity. He lived his life in a way that people knew he could be trusted. His lifestyle was the same at home; we knew him to be trustworthy—a man of his word.

Are you trustworthy, or is it time for change? Make sure your behavior is without question, no matter who is watching. Learn to be forthright, honest, and truthful, even if it gets you in trouble. You don't have to win every discussion and you can thoughtfully consider how you're impacting your companion. Being trustworthy will make it easy for your companion to enjoy your presence.

87. Look Into The Heart

What do you see when you look at your companion? A runway model or a plain Jane? The Hulk or Howdy Doody? A nag or an encouraging person? A socialite or an isolator? What do you see? What are you looking for?

Taking time to look into the heart can help you find the real person within, one with joys and heartbreaks, fun and sadness, failures and successes, likes and dislikes. It takes time and patience to get to know your companion and peer into the heart. Behavior is quickly observable, but knowing the person deeply and knowing the heart is much more tedious work. It requires that you overlook the flaws and hang-ups. Quirks and behavior will block your vision if you let them. If you focus so much on what you *don't* like, you'll miss what you *do* like. It's easy to get sidetracked by the negative, which tends to stand out.

To get to the heart, set aside your own agenda and avoid be self serving. Respect your companion without trying to change him or her. Appreciate the knowledge that your mate is one of a kind. There is no one else on earth like them. Even identical twins are each their own person. Each has his or her own personality. Cherish and value what you find and you might discover that the search never really ends. It's more of a journey than a destination.

Looking into the heart is a choice. Be intentional and pay attention. It's not a casual experience, but it pays huge dividends when you look into the heart of your companion.

88. Stay Out Of The Blame Game

So who's right and who's wrong? Does it matter that much? I suppose in certain situations it could be really important, but in most cases it matters very little. When we "feel like" issues are important, we might overreact. We can get so caught up in who's right and who's wrong that we forget what we began talking about. We then surf topics and focus on blaming the companion, instead of resolving the issue at hand.

Blaming doesn't help matters very much. In fact, it usually hurts the situation, rarely bringing resolution. Blaming your companion will only drive him or her away and make matters worse. Instead of blaming, try working together to resolve an issue. It matters little about who's right and who's wrong; what really matters is that we work together to see if we can deal with the issue at hand. Stick to the subject and take your time in looking for ways to handle the matter. Opt for solutions and understanding over correctness. When important matters are involved, pointing fingers rarely helps. Keep your head and find workable solutions instead of blaming.

One way to achieve this is to realize that you two are on the same side of the table and working to find a common solution. If you will spend your time working toward understanding and mutual solutions, you'll not lapse into blaming each other. Work together to resolve issues and stay out of the blame game.

89. Care About What Your Companion Cares About

It's important to understand that some things are a mountain to one person, but a molehill to the other. Something that your companion deems major may seem very minor to you. Study your companion to learn what's important to him or her.

"Caring about" what your companion enjoys doesn't mean that you enjoy it for yourself. It simply recognizes what it means to your companion. For example, my wife doesn't enjoy fishing, but she gives gift cards for fishing supplies for my birthday. She supports what I care about, even though she doesn't have much interest for herself.

Another angle to consider is what your companion is *not* interested in? For example, Linda is *not* interested in camping. I don't ask her to go camping because I know she has no interest in it and would be miserable at the campground. Understanding your companion's dislikes is as important as knowing his or her interests.

Get to know your companion's likes and dislikes. The more you understand and respect them, the more you'll learn to care about what he or she cares about. It's not necessary to like all of the same things. A relationship can work just fine without having everything in common. The key is to *care* about what your companion cares about. By doing this, you'll show your understanding, respect and love for your companion. It's well worth the energy and effort you'll invest.

90. Manage Your Attitude

A good attitude is fundamental for a healthy relationship. Your attitude will be reflected through your words, body language and tone of voice. Your attitude will reveal itself. You cannot be without an attitude, but can manage it, skewing it toward the good side. You have the choice of showing a good one or a poor one. And it is, indeed, a *choice*. Focusing on the negatives of life or injustices can lead to a poor attitude. On the other hand, focusing on the good and the lovely things of life can lead to a better one.

Attitude doesn't just *happen* to you and prohibit you from having power over it. A common mistake is to let your emotions determine your actions or attitude. Emotions come and go. Don't let your attitude passively ride the waves of your emotions. Take charge of it.

You manage your attitude by thinking issues through. The beauty of life and the ugly of it co-exist. They mingle together, so you live with both. You cannot get rid of the ugly things of life, but you do have the power to refrain from letting them take over.

Your attitude speaks volumes to your companion. It tells him or her whether you are pleased or disappointed. It reveals how you view them. Learning to manage your attitude will let you handle what life throws at you, rather than being managed by the circumstances of life. A good attitude will make some really important statements in your relationship.

91. Practice Good Personal Hygiene

A guy once told me that he didn't use deodorant. "Yep, I know", I replied. It was obvious. People know when you don't practice good personal hygiene; they can tell from thirty feet away.

Personal hygiene is a huge factor in a relationship. Do you really think your companion likes to snuggle up to you when you are sweaty and smelly? You don't have to become fanatic, but good personal hygiene is essential.

Good personal hygiene quietly feeds the relationship in a positive way. Brush your teeth, clip your nails and keep yourself presentable. Practicing good personal hygiene is about caring for you and taking a little healthy self-pride. Failure to care for and about yourself doesn't extend much consideration toward your companion.

We usually like attractive companions. We normally have an attraction (not all physical) for the one who will be our companion. It is wise to be thoughtful and *be* that attractive companion.

There are plenty of times to sweat, work hard, play hard and get downright dirty and filthy. After the fun or work is over, take a shower and get presentable for your companion. Have all the fun you can and work as hard as you like—those are important components of life—but then clean up and get ready for time with your companion.

Good hygiene is about being thoughtful to your companion. It's about being presentable and pleasant to be near. Your companion will appreciate it when you are.

92. Give Respect

Every person needs respect. Who better to give it to your companion than you? Respect builds a sense of well being and personal value. We rarely need to say "I respect you"; it's better *shown* by action and attitude. We show respect by listening to understand and care. We express respect with a warm tone of voice when we communicate, with facial expressions that are caring and concerned and with body language that is engaging. Showing respect is a matter of the heart, which expresses itself in many forms.

You can't fake respect. You can try, but that becomes manipulation. Manipulation is a huge form of disrespect. Examine your heart to make sure you are giving respect for who your companion is, rather than for what you might gain.

Respect has to do with seeing your companion as a valuable person that deserves all the best from you. Your companion deserves your attention, your care, your nurturing, and your greatest support. Be your companion's greatest supporter.

You give respect by noticing your companion's assets and strengths. It's difficult to show respect when you focus on weaknesses and flaws. All of us have flaws, but we also have strengths. A guy once told me that he'd spent years making his wife into the woman he wanted her to be. Now that she's become that woman, he doesn't like her anymore. Instead of making your companion into the person you want him or her to be, try respecting who they *are*. Respecting your companion, by the way you treat him or her, will say "I love you".

93. See Your Companion As A Person

Most of us start out okay with seeing our companion as a person, but in some cases, it doesn't remain that way for very long. With some, unfortunately, a companion can become viewed as a servant, a maid, a punching bag, a sugar daddy, a gofer (go for this, go for that), a piece of furniture, a door mat, etc. How do you see your companion? Do you see your companion existing in your life only to meet your needs?

Learn to see your companion as a person who has likes and dislikes, dreams and ideas, thoughts and opinions. If you fail to see them as a real person, you may begin to see him or her as a stumbling block to your ideas—as someone who gets in the way, as you try to achieve something.

Value your companion as a person who deserves all the respect and honor you can give, who is valuable and important; not just someone who's there to support you. In today's world, there are a number of people who don't feel like they're valued as a person, but simply used for what they can do or provide. Don't let your companion feel that way. Make sure that your actions, words and attitude fully express that you see your companion as a valued person.

Sometimes we're too busy to stop and consider others. As you ponder the value of your companion as a person, you'll notice all sorts of strengths and abilities. You'll see him or her as someone fully deserving of respect, consideration and recognition. If you fail to see your companion as a real person, you may soon fail to see them at all.

94. Prepare A Warm Bath For Your Companion

What a romantic idea! Sometimes it's purely a practical or thoughtful task. If your companion has had a really tough or stressful day, it could be a way to let her soak away the stress and relax for awhile. Or maybe you could grab that novel, place it beside the tub, and let her relax for no reason at all.

The idea is to give a gift to your companion, just because you care. There are thoughtful things you can do, which have a gentle way of showing that you are in-touch with, and are thinking about, your companion. Come up with a list of ideas that might help your companion relax.

Life takes on a rhythm that lulls us into believing the notion that things need to always be efficient and productive. Sometimes we need to set life's activities aside and relax for a little while. Sometimes we just need a nap. Life's not all work and no play. There are times to achieve production and efficiency and there are times for rest and relaxation. Providing for moments of relaxation for your companion will speak volumes about how much you care. Your creativity can take you far beyond a warm bath. For example, getting things done around the house will make it easier for your companion to sit down and relax. Picking up after yourself will prevent your adding even more things to your companion's to-do list, before they're able to relax.

Preparing a warm bath may require a little effort on your part, but healthy relationships require such effort and thoughtfulness. There's little room for autopilot in a healthy relationship. Keep your brain in the "on" position if you want to send the message of "I love you".

95. Allow For Imperfection

Perfection is really cool if you're having brain surgery. Or, if you're going to the moon, you'll probably want perfectly accurate calculations. However, for most of your life, perfection is not necessarily required, nor should it be expected. Surely, in relationships, perfection will not happen very often. Truth is, we're just not that good. Neither you nor your companion will get it all right. Whether its communication, bringing home the groceries, paying the bills or clipping the grass, give some latitude for mistakes and mess-ups.

We all make mistakes. Learn to develop a tolerance for your companion and rearrange your expectations, so that perfection is not the goal. Your companion will know if you're holding the standard too high and you'll become easily disappointed by doing so. Stop and survey areas in which you might be expecting perfection. Could it be appearance, performance, personality style, socializing, etc.? Maybe it's not just in your companion that you expect perfection, but from yourself? You could be driving your companion crazy because you expect perfection not from them, but you.

Excellence is a great goal, but perfection is unnecessary and unreasonable in most situations. Set reasonable goals and standards. Expect things to be done well, but question if you're really expecting perfection. If so, try adjusting your expectations to a more reasonable level. Allow for both of you to be human and have flexibility when it's needed. Work toward quality, but allow for humanity.

96. Take Your Companion A Glass Of Tea

If your companion is busy or thirsty, get a glass of tea for him or her. It's a powerful thing to *notice* what your companion needs and *do it*, without being asked. It's even more powerful to do something just because you want to, even if it is not a huge need; you do it just because you want to. Anything can stand in for the glass of tea. There are thousands of things that you could do for your companion that will say "I love you". The idea is to do something for your companion "just because". You don't *have* to, but you *want* to. I couldn't tell you how many times Linda has brought to me a glass of tea, a protein bar or snack, while I was working outside. I rarely have to ask; she always seems to know when I could use one.

When you do something for your companion, it conveys the notion that you're thinking about him or her; it reveals that you're in touch. There is nothing that says "I love you" quite like being in-touch enough to anticipate what your companion needs or wants. Begin to notice what your companion needs and just do it.

Expand your thinking on the subject. It could be a glass of tea, a task like doing the towels, a flower, a day trip, keeping the kids while your companion gets a break, washing the car, polishing her shoes, cleaning the countertops, getting that project finished or sitting down to relax together. I hope you're getting the picture. It's all about being in-touch with what your companion needs or wants. Study your mate to learn what he or she would enjoy. You might find thousands of little things you can do to say "I love you".

97. Don't Try To Fix Your Companion

Your companion is not broken and doesn't need to be fixed. When you're with someone long enough, you see their quirks, notice things that irritate you and observe things that they do that don't work so well. All of us have quirks and dysfunctional behaviors. The last thing your companion needs is for you to try to fix him or her. It's easy to make the mistake of trying to change each other when, in fact, the only person you can change is you.

When you're trying to fix your companion, you're sending the message that something is wrong with him or her and you know best how to fix it. You might have good intentions, but that doesn't make it work any better. Your motivation may be something like not wanting them to be seen in a negative light or to be embarrassed. Regardless of the intentions, trying to fix or change your companion will have a negative effect and outcome.

Learn to accept your companion for who he or she is. You'll discover a huge bundle of positive characteristics and some negative ones. Allow the quirks and neat things to co-exist. None of us are perfect or without quirks. Just love your companion and don't try to fix them. Learning to love your companion for who they are will be a huge step toward conveying the notion of "I love you". You probably don't want your companion to fix you, so return the favor by resisting the temptation to do the same to him or her.

98. Let Her Sleep

Sometimes you just need to let her (or him) sleep. All of us get worn out and sometimes need to catch up a little. Life does that to us; it brings us to the point of exhaustion and we just need to remedy it with peaceful, restful sleep.

Of course, we need to tend to important matters and pay the bills. Tasks need to be completed, in order to make life work well. There are a million things that need to be done and we should be diligent in tending to those things on a regular basis. In fact, *not* tending to the important things will actually hinder your rest and make you even more tired. However, sometimes we simply need a break. Rearrange your own mental furniture to make it okay for your companion to rest for awhile when needed.

Different agendas can be frustrating. Your own agenda seems reasonable to you. Your companion's agenda might not seem as much so, but it certainly does to him or her. Needs that seem reasonable and logical to one person may be seem totally different to another, even if that need is as simple as a restful nap. Take time to figure out what is needed at the time.

Rest does wonders. A well-rested companion is usually more pleasant than a tired one. Which do you prefer? One of the kindest things you can do is to be in touch with your companion enough to realize that he or she has needs and be helpful in fulfilling those needs. So let him or her sleep and protect the environment to provide some down time when needed.

99. Pay Attention

Paying attention is a huge "I love you". Pay attention to what your companion is saying and to what's important to him or her. Pay attention to what needs to be done and to the schedule and important events. Pay attention to family matters. You get the picture: pay attention.

A quick way to shout "I don't care!" is to fail to pay attention. This can happen easily by becoming dependent on your companion to remind you of important events, the to-do list, etc. Don't delegate the things that you should be doing or taking care of. Don't get a snack, leave stuff on the kitchen counter and then walk out of the room, like it is none of your concern. You may think someone else will take care of it—they probably will—but you're sending a message that you don't care.

How well do you take care of business? Take an inventory. Do you keep things running smoothly or do you leave a wake of things for others to handle? How well do you tend to matters as they come up? If you need to grow in this area, start with what's right in front of you. Pick up your coffee cup and take it to the dishwasher. Get out the bills and pay them. Mow the lawn and hose off the patio. Take a look around, notice what needs to be done, and take care of business.

Pay attention to your companion's emotions and needs. They can give you important clues about things that might need to be done. Paying attention: what a way to say "I love you"!

100. Problem Solve

Some people are quick to solve a problem, or at least tell you how you ought to handle it. However, we don't always want someone just giving a solution or telling us how we should handle something. Step back and think first; ask yourself if this is a time to listen and care. Is it clearly a time that requires problem solving? Don't necessarily go with your feelings, because those feelings can lead you to wrong conclusions. If you solve problems all day long, you'll likely see *every* issue as one that needs solving. If the only tool you have in your box is a hammer, you'll see everything as a nail.

If there's truly an issue that needs resolution, work together to deal with it. Take your time and slow down the process. Listen, so you can get the whole picture, instead of going with only what you see. Value what your companion offers. See if you can comprehend the matter from his or her viewpoint, to gain fresh perspective. Pool your thoughts and work together. Brainstorm ideas to come up with solutions that will incorporate concerns that each of you have. Some of the best solutions will be joint efforts.

Now, on the down side…If you procrastinate and never get around to the hard issues of life, or if you avoid conflict at all cost, you might notice your relationship start to distance. Unresolved issues create gaps between companions. Peace, at any price, ends up being no peace at all. Don't be afraid to resolve issues, but view them as opportunities to work together to come to grips with important matters. Working together to solve problems can actually bring you closer together.

101. Get Help

Nobody's perfect. We all have flaws. You will not find the perfect companion, nor will you be the perfect companion. We don't expect relationships to be without difficulties, but work to make them better and enjoyable.

Sometimes we need help. Unfortunately, most of us aren't taught how to have a good relationship. For some reason, people are expected to just know how to relate. They tend to go about it by repeating what they've seen or heard. Clichés abound regarding relationships, but they don't usually work and often make matters worse.

There's plenty of help available. Bookstores are loaded with resources that will help you to build a healthy relationship. Don't like to read? Many books are available in audio form, so you can listen instead. There are seminars, conferences and classes available out there to enrich your relationship.

There are counselors who are trained to help you with relationship issues, as well as personal ones. If your personal issues are damaging your relationship or hindering you from healthy, interactional practices, seek help to work through them. Don't put it off; get help now. A true professional can better guide you. Getting help requires work, but its well worth it in the long run. The stigma is fading about getting professional help. People are finding that it's honorable to seek help when needed and that it's unwise to think they can do it alone. All of us need help from time to time. Be bold. If you need help, ask and you'll find someone who will gladly offer it.

The Challenge

Now that you've breezed through 101 relationship builders, it's time to come up with a few of your own. Think about what your companion might like. Write them down and figure out a way to provide them for him or her. This should be an organic list, since people change over time, developing new and fresh preferences.

More importantly, become intentional about being thoughtful of your companion. Doing so will help you implement these and other ideas. It's so easy to read information and have the best of intentions, but if you don't put into practice what you learn, none of it will translate into behavioral change. Sometimes we're more a creature of habit than we prefer to be. Without a change-of-mind, you're likely to revert back to the old way of thinking, failing to apply what you know. Knowing is not enough. You will need to develop a plan to *implement* what you know. The plan must be put into action.

Take time to think through how you might best develop a system of putting these practices in place. Figure out what works best for you. It's necessary to start with *a desire* to build a healthy relationship with your companion. You must find a way to regularly think about what you'll do to convey your love, and how you'll do it. Don't try to put thirty items into practice at a time; it's better to start with one or two. Work on those until you're good at them, then add another and then another. Working on a few items at a time will help you build good habits.

Practicing healthy relationship principles will bring more enjoyment to your relationship.

Made in the USA
Charleston, SC
26 January 2014